Gandhian Thought:
New World, New Dimensions

GANDHIAN THOUGHT:
NEW WORLD, NEW DIMENSIONS

RAVINDRA KUMAR

Publications

KALPAZ PUBLICATIONS
DELHI-110052

Gandhian Thought: New World, New Dimensions

ISBN: 81-7835-644-9

Published in 2008 in India by
Kalpaz Publications
C-30, Satyavati Nagar, Delhi-110052
Ph: 9212729499
Email: kalpaz@hotmail.com

Lasertype Setting by: Kumar
Printed at: Salasar Imaging System, Delhi

To

Candice C Carter

Contents

Foreword

In late September and early October 2007, the University of North Florida, collaborating with organizations such as the Gandhi Memorial Society of Jacksonville, hosted a Peace Awareness Week and a Symposium on Conflict Resolution. As part of these events, we were fortunate to have Dr. Ravindra Kumar, an award-winning Indologist, scholar and educator, join us. During his time on campus and in our community, Dr. Kumar delivered several public addresses, which serve as the basis for this text on Mahatma Gandhi's teachings.

While each of Dr. Kumar's speeches stands by itself, as a collective body these seven works offer insights on the depth and breadth of the Mahatma's teachings, challenging the reader to understand both the meaning and continuing importance of Gandhi's life and writings. Dr. Kumar also makes clear that Gandhi sought to offer his message to all humankind, not just to those who were engaged in the struggles of colonial India.

In individual speeches, Dr. Kumar presents Gandhi's teachings on various topics including the challenges of democracy and the resolution of international conflict. He also points to individuals across the world, who have taken Gandhi's call seriously to use the pursuit of Truth [***Satyagraha***] and Non-Violence [***Ahimsa***] as the tools of change, helping us to recognize that in following this path these individuals have shown an enduring willingness to understand and accommodate 'the other' while maintaining an unfailing commitment to Gandhian principles.

Those who were able to spend time with Dr. Kumar while he was with us in Florida were enlightened by his presentations. I am confident that readers of these essays after their publication in a book form titled ***'Gandhian Thought: New World, New Dimensions'*** will also be enriched in their pursuit of peace.

Jacksonville, FL
[USA]

-John A Delaney
President,
University of North Florida

Introduction

Mahatma Gandhi's role and contribution to India's Freedom Movement is noteworthy, extraordinary and exemplary. Those who are familiar with the events of the National Liberation Movement of India know how Gandhi awakened the masses through the strength of ***Ahimsa*** [non-violence]; by utilizing ***Satyagraha***, the best and most infallible weapon, he made the people realize the value of independence and called upon them to cut their centuries-old chains of slavery. The people of India came to the forefront in response, and ultimately in the year 1947 India became free from the Imperial Rule of the English.

Here one important thing comes to my mind time and again, and it is my duty to clarify it. Most people consider India's political freedom to be the goal of Mahatma Gandhi's life. They think his aim was to set his country free from the English, and it is but natural if people think so. Mahatma Gandhi spent most of his life striving to make his nation politically free; for 25 years [1917-1942] he led his compatriots explicitly for explicit purpose; he spent more than ten years in various prisons of the British Empire while fighting for freedom of India. Nevertheless, in spite of the fact that the first goal of Mahatma Gandhi's life was to achieve freedom for India, it was not at all the end of his mission.

For, it was so, how could Gandhi still be considered a ray of hope by millions around the world? How could he has become the source of inspiration for Martin Luther King Jr., Nelson Mandela, Ninoy Aquino, Bisweshwar Prasad Koirala and other great people of the world? How could he even today inspire countries like Thailand, where people carrying Mahatma Gandhi's pictures in their hands, protest on the streets? It clearly indicates that life, work and views of Mahatma Gandhi were for the welfare of whole of humanity; the way he showed through his dynamic actions was, and is, for the entire world; India's freedom was only a dimension of his way.

Hence, those who consider India's freedom to be the only goal of Mahatma Gandhi's life must review their opinion by familiarizing themselves with the Mahatma's philosophy and his actions dedicated to his belief in the synthetic whole, which is the unity of human life.

II

Two thousand five hundred years ago, it was Gautama the Buddha, who for the first time in the Indian Sub-Continent, by emphasizing on reality of the ***Law of Change***, called upon humanity to break the bonds, which enslave people at different levels and different planes. He showed the masses the best way to rid themselves of their problems and to lead life based on equality, peace and prosperity. At the same time, he asserted that even what he said at the time was not beyond the process of the ***Law of Change***, for nothing could be the exception. This meant that even what the Buddha said and suggested for the welfare of mankind could not be one hundred percent applied in the times to come. However, the Buddha's way, teachings and suggestions can even today become a source of inspiration, if they are applied according to the demands of time and space. This is the height of his achievement, for which he is rightly called the ***Light of Asia***.

Besides ***Shakyamuni*** Gautama, it was Mahatma Gandhi whose mass actions based on ***Ahimsa*** [non-violence] became the source of inspiration for many in the world. If Gandhi's welfaristic and exemplary standards are applied today, according to the prevailing conditions of time and space, they are fully capable of bringing unique and beautiful results to humanity. For this reason Mohandas Karamchand Gandhi was elevated to the stature of a Mahatma. People around the world respect him; they look at his exemplary actions and with these in hand, they try to rid the world of its problems and conflicts at different levels and planes.

III

In this manuscript entitled, ***'Gandhian Thought: New World, New Dimensions'***, seven of my lectures regarding different aspects of Mahatma Gandhi's life and philosophy, delivered at the University of North Florida, Jacksonville, USA have been included. I hope that after publication, this manuscript will be useful to those who are interested in Mahatma Gandhi's life, works and views.

I express my gratitude to the authorities of the University of North Florida, especially President Mr. John A Delaney, who also contributed a Foreword for this work; Dr. Mauricio Gonzalez, Vice President for Student and International Affairs; Dr. Tom Serwartka, Vice President and Chief of the Staff; Professor Candice C Carter of the College of Education and

Human Services, to whom I have dedicated this work; Professor John Frank and Professor Henry Thomas, of the Political Science Department; and Mr. Oupa Seane, Director of the Intercultural Center for Peace. I would also like to express my appreciation to the Gandhi Memorial Society of Jacksonville, Florida, particularly Mr. Ramesh Vashi, Chairman and Mr. Ashok Bazaz, the President, for having given me the opportunity to express my views on various aspects of Mahatma Gandhi's life, work and philosophy. I also convey my thanks to Ms. Ana Linares, Ms. Lorna Bautista, Ms. Christine Bender, Ms. Damala Simon, Ms. Azalia Torres, Mr. Omololu Ogunlewe and Mr. Sachin Bathla for their help in typing and reading the proofs of this manuscript.

I especially convey my sincere thanks to Ms. Shirley "Sunny" Guiron, who has extended all her cooperation in the final preparation of this manuscript before sending it for publication.

Meerut [India] **-Ravindra Kumar**

25th October 2007

1

Satyagraha, Conflict-Transformation and a Sustainable Culture of Peace

"Satyragraha is a Dharmayuddha, one of the most powerful methods of direct action; it is a force that [though] works silently and apparently slowly [but] in reality, there is no force in the world that is so direct or so swift in working; it excludes every form of violence, veiled or unveiled, and whether in thought, word of deed."

-MK Gandhi

Satyagraha, Its Birth and Power

People acquainted with the life and works of Mahatma Gandhi know that during the last decade of the Nineteenth Century, he was drawn into South African struggle because the domiciled Indian immigrants there suffered from many political, economic and social injustices. He, therefore, engaged himself in search of a method and technique of resistance to remove these inequities. However, Gandhi also wished that this technique must operate within the domain of fundamental moral principles.

Thus, the method of resistance that Mahatma Gandhi developed to end various social, political and economic wrongs was first applied in South Africa during the last decade of the Nineteenth Century and the first two decades of the Twentieth Century. His campaigns for truth, justice and fairness further evolved over time and were carried-out on a wider scale in India between 1917 and 1942, from Champaran to Quit India Movement. Gandhi's campaigns for justice were assigned many names, i.e., Passive Resistance, Non-Cooperation, Civil Disobedience or the Salt Movement, etc. However, Mahatma Gandhi was uncomfortable with those terms as they did not fully convey the ethical, moral and spiritual aspects of his struggles. He, therefore, termed his methods ***Satyagraha***, which means ***The Pursuit of Truth***.

To Mahatma Gandhi it is a restless search for Truth and determination to reach Truth.[1]

In practice, ***Satyagraha,*** that is also an ***Ahimsak*** fight [non-violent struggle] of Mahatma Gandhi, is perhaps the most courageous and glorious experiment ever made by a person in the entire human history.

Generally, ***Satyagraha*** can be legitimately offered by a person, who respects the rule of law and otherwise obeys law. However, in fact, a ***Satyagrahi***-a person in search of truth-refuses to obey the law that he believes is wrong and immoral. By refusing to obey such a law he paradoxically respects the rule of law by accepting the extreme penalty set for the so-called offence. In essence, a ***Satyagrahi*** respects the law, but offers non-cooperation in regards to its evil elements only.

According to Mahatma Gandhi, ***Satyagraha*** should be based on the principles of love, mutual cooperation and understanding-the foundation of existence and progress. Because such a quest incorporates sincerity, respect and restraint, ***Satyagraha*** requires utmost patience, the highest faith, and the willingness to suffer great humiliation. On this path, all are brothers. For, there is no place for ill-will or hatred in the search for Truth. Furthermore, ***Satyagraha*** also rejects the idea of physical struggle, and it should not be pre-planned; for to Mahatma Gandhi a struggle, which has been previously planned, is not a righteous struggle.

"Satyragraha", in view of Mahatma Gandhi himself, ***"is a Dharmayuddha, one of the most powerful methods of direct action*** [2]***; it is a force that [though] works silently and apparently slowly [but] in reality, there is no force in the world that is so direct or so swift in working;***[3] ***it excludes every form of violence, veiled or unveiled, and whether in thought, word of deed."***[4]

A man with ***Satya*** [truth] and ***Ahimsa*** [non-violence] through ***Satyagraha*** can bring the world to his feet, because he accepts and adopts Truth as a principle as well as the way of life. And, definitely it was the power of ***Satyagraha***, on the basis of which Gandhi succeeded to get the ***Black Act*** and ***Immigration Act*** abolished in South Africa; simultaneously, he became successful in getting removed the provision of ***Pound-3 Tax*** imposed on each and every Indian and other Asians there.

What Mahatma Gandhi claimed in respect of power and strength of ***Satyagraha*** that again proved to be true in various ***Satyragrahas*** [non-violent struggles], launched for the freedom of India under his own leadership, on the strength of which he not only transformed India into a nation by uniting people and that resulted in creating a will amongst his compatriots to live together, which meant sharing weal and woe, but he also successfully lead his countrymen to the door of freedom from centuries old slavery.

Ahimsa-the Means of *Satyagraha*

Ahimsa [non-violence], that is the opposite state of violence in toto, and the source of all human values including love and cooperation, and one of the two sides of that coin, of which ***Satya*** [truth] is the other side, is the means of ***Satyagraha***. ***Ahimsa*** [non-violence] and truth are intertwined, and according to Mahatma Gandhi:

"It is impossible to disentangle and separate them. They are...rather of a smooth unstamped metallic disk. Who can say which the obverse is and which is the reverse? Nevertheless ahimsa is the means; truth is the end."[5]

Satyagrahi

One who is a ***Satyagrahi*** [a seeker of truth], he must be humble. Truth is not denominational. It is neither yours nor mine. It knows no frontiers. Therefore, ***"A Satyagrahi"***, as Mahatma Gandhi says, ***"exhausts all other means before he resorts to Satyagraha."***[6]

And:

"He will, therefore, constantly and continually approach the constituted authority, he will appeal to public opinion, educate public opinion, state his case calmly and coolly before everybody who wants to listen him and only after he has exhausted all these avenues he will resort to Satyagraha. But when he has found the impelling call of the inner voice within him and launches out upon Satyagraha he has burnt his boats and there is no receding."[7]

Further, it is necessary for a ***Satyagrahi*** that in the pursuit of truth, he must not admit violence against his opponent, but he must be weaned from error by patience and sympathy; he should be ready for self-suffering and must not wish of opponent's suffering.

Transformation of Conflict into Cooperation

Conflict, like cooperation, is inevitable in human society; it is but natural in day-to-day practices. This has been true for thousands of years; histories of ancient, medieval and contemporary periods are before us to prove this fact. Why is this so? In spite of cooperation that operates fully within the domain of ***Ahimsa*** [non-violence-an eternal value permanently present in human nature, or supplemental to it], through the ages, due to competition and jealousy [two temporary tendencies of man], selfishness, appetites and passions develop in him. To satisfy his desires he wishes to become master of others, which gives birth to the state of conflict at different levels in social, political or economic spheres. The same things apply in the context of a community, society or nation. A community, society or nation is made of men, for what is true of a man is true of a community, society or nation.

However it is cooperation that ultimately records victory over conflict-not only in the life of an individual, but in the lives of communities, societies and nations. In other words, conflicts are always transformed into cooperation. If this were not so, the unprecedented growth of progress made in various walks of life by man and his institutions would never have been made possible.

It is said that in his primitive, undeveloped age, man was absolutely like a wild animal. He, along with others, wandered here and there. Men killed one another to satisfy their appetite. Generally, they too became the victims of wild animals. In such a state there was a question mark on their very existence.

This state of affairs underwent a change. At the root of this change was man's idea of the safety of his existence. Instead of killing and eating one another, man began to kill and eat only animals. Even then, however, his existence could not be assured.

As the ideas formulating in man's mind matured, the spirit of collectivity consequently developed. Instead of wandering here and there, man decided to inhabit one place. By doing so, men found themselves more secure from the attacks of wild animals. If an animal or a group of animals attacked, the group of men, dwelling at one place, could counter the attack collectively. Therefore, it was definitely the spirit of cooperation that ensured their collective safety and survival.

For some time this state of affairs continued. Then man's thinking further developed to add a new dimension. Instead of killing wild animals to fill-up his belly, man started domesticating them. This led man to achieve two chief benefits of a unique nature. First: man received milk as nectar; and second: domestic animals proved helpful in agricultural work as well as becoming the best means of transport.

Due to man's domestication of animals, and using them for agricultural and other purposes, it was only natural that their killing decreased. Instead of meat, agricultural products became man's main source of daily food. Many other changes also took place in this regard, and if we want to be familiar with them, we can analyze man's long historical journey. However, what I can say in brief is that whatever final situation is before us today is due to victory of cooperation over conflicts.

I have discussed above that in the process of ensuring mankind's existence, progressive ideas arose in men's minds and, consequently, the spirit of collectivity emerged in them. I also talked of their dwelling together with unity at a specific place instead of wandering here and there. Now, I want to reiterate that it was also due to continuation of this very process of development and change, due to victory of cooperation over conflicts that clans, families, villages, towns, cities and major cities surcharged with manifold facilities also became part and parcel of it.

The process of change that began when man first ensured the safety of his existence continued as he joined in friendship with many animals through their domestication. Passing through this never-ending process of development, man continued to advance further towards the achievement of his goals. This confirms that despite temporary tendencies that give birth to conflicts, cooperation under the patronage of non-violence is permanently present in human nature, and neither in the absence of which men can live united nor come within the domain of collectivity. Furthermore, if they did not have collectivity in life, their existence would not have remained intact, not to mention progress or the achievement of goals, for, as Mahatma Gandhi rightly pointed out, ***"Mankind would have been self-destroyed ages ago."***[8]

We were talking of victory of cooperation over conflicts, or transformation of conflicts into cooperation. In this context, we should keep in mind that morality, also one of the principal supplementary values of ***Ahimsa*** [non-violence], and one of the three chief fundamentals of civilization[9], has been present even in ancient times and throughout the ages in the social behaviours of men. And as JB Kripalani rightly points out, in comparison to political morality, social morality has been far more advanced, especially inter-group morality[10], which plays an important role in the process of transformation of conflicts into cooperation in social life. Even today, it can be observed that irregardless of whether we follow the moral conducts or violate them due to selfishness, passion or appetites, we ultimately recognize the validity of social life and behaviours [which are based upon mutual trust, or cooperation or ***Ahimsa***-non-violence], praising those who follow it and condemning those who do not.

In the political sphere the above state of affairs has been quite different. Here, due to lack of morality, selfishness [including the wish for economic gains], distrust and hatred make the situation more serious and complicated. This leads not only to conflicts, but to severe violence as well as war, where might alone is right, where the law of the jungle rules, where groups and nations in their relations consider one another as political enemies. None of them steps forward to sacrifice for the other, unlike the social sphere, where on many occasions individuals are ready to sacrifice their own self-interests.

But, if unlike the social sphere, there is a lack of morality in the political field, can we not transform conflicts into cooperation? Can we not create a culture of peace there? Yes, we definitely can.

We know that in the entire human history, great men[11] have made efforts in this direction. The prime example is Mahatma Gandhi, who, especially in the Twentieth Century, called upon people to foster political and economic fields with morality, so that all conflicts, whether local, national, or international, could be transformed into cooperation and a healthy atmosphere for a sustainable culture of peace is created. We are also aware of the fact that Mahatma Gandhi was firm about the application of sincere cooperation and non-violence in political and economic spheres, as well as the social sphere. In this regard his views and practices are fully capable to guide us even today. The powerfully unique and exemplary weapon of ***Satyagraha*** as outlined by Gandhi, is more than relevant to end any kind of injustice and create a sustainable culture of peace in these days of globalization, where people of the world share their common interests and come in close contact with one another, if it is applied honestly, according to the need of time and space.

The Way to Create a Sustainable Culture of Peace

Mahatma Gandhi, influenced by the ***Vedic-Hindu*** doctrine that ***"All life is one"***[12] and also the Christian concept that ***"we are members one of another"***[13] believed that human life and society are in a sense organic; that human life, individual and group, social, economic and political cannot be divided into separate and airtight compartments.[14] He considered all creatures from one and the same God, and made Him the basis of oneness by saying:

"Man should earnestly desire well-being of all God's creation and pray that he might have the strength to do so. In desiring the well-being of all lies his own welfare; he who desires only his own or his community's welfare is selfish and it can never be well with him."[15]

What is good in social behaviours is also good in political and economic relations; if morality and ethics are welfaristic in the social field then they are equally welfaristic in other fields also. The problem has been that we adopt a double standard when we apply ***Ahimsa*** [non-violence], or other values supplementary to it, in the political field. At times like this we definitely forget the concept of oneness, as mentioned above. We, knowingly or unknowingly, also forget the message of Mahatma Gandhi, in which he said:

"You cannot divide life, social, economic, political and purely religious, into watertight compartments. I do not know of any religion apart from human activity. It provides a moral basis of all other activities, which they would otherwise lack, reducing life to a maze of sound and fury signifying nothing."[16]

We preferably try to solve problems related to social life through non-violence and activities related to it; we try to take the course of morality there, come ahead to cooperate, but in other fields, especially the political field, we interact in a different way. The situation becomes more complicated and serious when a problem relates to international politics. Then the parties involved resolve the issue through the use of violence or even indulge in a war-like conflict and by doing so they forget that a conflict or war has never accorded a permanent and peaceful solution to the problem. Rather, conflicts that have been attempted to solve by the use of violence create more conflicts of a complicated nature. The example of the World War Second is particularly before us to prove this fact.

As I have said earlier, conflicts are inevitable in the day-to-day behaviours or practices of human society or in different walks of life at different levels, no matter if they are temporary in nature. But, side-by-side, they demand resolution; or in other words, they demand their transformation into cooperation.

Taking it as necessary for human life, we should accord them a solution in a noble way, and as I believe, the unique character and way of ***Satyagraha*** as outlined by Mahatma Gandhi is the best one, the application of which in political and economic fields cannot be underestimated. As this very way is based upon principles, it involves a largest interest of people; simultaneously, it can be a moral substitute to war.

Satyagraha in Democracy

Satyagraha, as one of the most powerful methods of direct action, is fully capable in a democratic setting to restore freedom and seek justice at the local and national level in social, political and economic spheres. In a democracy people have full rights to aim for ***Satyagraha*** if justice is denied, or individual as well as community freedom is snatched. And steps like ***Non-Cooperation*** and ***Civil Disobedience*** can be taken according to the circumstances of time and space.

Satyagraha in International Sphere

But, as far as the question of application of ***Satyagraha*** in the international sphere is concerned, in my opinion, it is possible through certain steps, especially if ***Non-Cooperation***, ***Boycott*** or ***Restriction*** is enacted with extra care, sincerity and honesty. Furthermore, these types of steps call for bigger responsibilities. For example, if there emerges a situation like that in Kuwait, in which some years ago Iraq tried to destroy its sovereignty, the responsibility of the international community becomes important. And it becomes even more important when a group of compatriots such as in Burma

[Myanmar] is bent on snatching away the democratic rights of the people.

Today, not a single country in the world is in a position to maintain its existence or to function in isolation, no matter how mighty it is. Countries are so interdependent that to act united has become compulsory. In such a state it is not possible even for a country whose dictators snatch the people's freedom to ignore the international call. Through a collective decision in the ***UNO*** the dictators of such a country may be first warned of a ***Non-Violent Non-Cooperation*** and ***Boycott including Restrictions***, and if there is no success in these tactics then under the leadership of ***UNO*** further steps can be taken according to conditions of time and space, keeping in mind the safety and difficulties of innocent people.

Such types of actions are, in fact, under the domain of non-violence; they are forward steps of ***Satyagraha***, because there is no ill-will in it. For ***Satyagraha*** means pursuit of Truth; it is the search for Truth and a determination to reach Truth by means of ***Ahimsa*** [non-violence] that is the only means to create a sustainable culture of peace. Hence, if it is applied in the international sphere, its outcome will definitely be benevolent and welfaristic.

References:

1. Young India, 19 March 1925
2. Ibid, 10 October 1927
3. Ibid, 4 June 1925
4. Harijan, 15 April 1933
5. Gandhi, MK, In Search of the Supreme, page 27

6. Young India, 10 October 1927
7. Ibid
8. Ibid, 2 January 1930
9. The other two fundamentals of civilization are: Non-violence and Freedom.
10. Gandhi: His Life and Thoughts, page 346
11. Like Gautama the Buddha, Socrates, Confucius, Tolstoy etc.
12. To say the Vedantic view
13. Gandhi: His Life and Thoughts, page 345
14. Ibid
15. Ibid, page 346
16. Ibid

Bibliography:

- Gandhi, MK, An Autobiography or The Story of My Experiments with Truth, Navajivan Publishing House, Ahmedabad, Gujarat [India], 1957
- Gandhi, MK, Harijan Weekly, Published Under the Auspices of Harijan Sewak-Sangh [1933-41]; by Navajivan Trust, Ahmedabad [India], Between 1942-48
- Gandhi, MK, India of My Dreams, Navajivan Publishing House, Ahmedabad, Gujarat [India], 1957 and Seventh Reprint, 1999
- Gandhi, MK, Young India Weekly [1919-1931], Reprinted in 13 Volumes by Navajivan Publishing House, Ahmedabad [India], 1984
- Kripalani, JB, Gandhi: His Life and Thought, Publications Division, Ministry of Information and Broadcasting, Government of India, New Delhi [India], 1991
- Kumar, Ravindra, Champaran to Quit India Movement, Mittal Publications, New Delhi [India], 2002

- Kumar, Ravindra, Essays on Gandhism and Peace, Krishna Publications, Meerut, Uttar Pradesh [India], 1999
- Kumar, Ravindra, Theory and Practice of Gandhian Non-Violence, Mittal Publications, New Delhi [India], 2002
- Prabhu, RK, & Rao UR, The Mind of Mahatma Gandhi, Navajivan Publishing House, Ahmedabad, Gujarat [India], 1967
- Sharp Gene, The Politics of Non-violent Action, Part 1-3, Boston [USA], 1973
- Tendulkar, DG, Mahatma: Life of Mohandas Karamchand Gandhi, 8 Volumes, VK Jhaveri and DG Tendulkar, Bombay [India], 1951-54
- Tolstoy, Leo, On Civil Disobedience and Non-Violence, A Signet Books, The American Library [USA], 1968

****

2

Gandhi's Philosophy of *Ahimsa* and its Application to Current International Conflicts

"Ahimsa cannot be dismissed as lightly as you think. Ahimsa is the strongest force known. But if all can use the strongest force with equal ease, it would lose its importance. We have not been able yet to discover the true measure of the innumerable properties of an article of our daily use like water. Some of its properties fill us with wonder. Let us not, therefore, make light of the strongest force like Ahimsa, and let's try to discover its hidden power with patience and faith."

-MK Gandhi

Philosophy of Gandhi

The best or essential part of Mahatma Gandhi's philosophy can be grasped from his statement:

"The whole gamut of man's activities…constitutes an indivisible whole. You cannot divide life, social, economic, political and purely religious, into watertight compartments…"

This clearly indicates that Mahatma Gandhi influenced by ***Vedantic*** doctrine that ***'all life is one'***, believed in the unity of human life. This unity is a synthetic whole and can neither be divided into separate social, religious, political, moral or ethical spheres; nor can it be differentiated by levels such as individual versus collective. What seem to be separate segments are, in fact, different facets of human life; they are inter-related, and act and react upon one another. The division of activities of human life into different compartments is artificial and is totally far from the reality.

God or the ***Supreme Being***, who is the ***Creator*** of all and called by different names, is the power behind the above unity. For Gandhi, ***He*** is also the ***'Truth'***[1] and it is ***His*** voice within everyone that serves as inspiration to follow the vision of ***Truth***, which is possible only by complete realization of ***Ahimsa*** [non-violence].[2] Thus, taking ***God***-the ***Supreme Being*** as the ***Creator*** of all, Mahatma Gandhi declared ***Him*** the ***Truth*** and the basis as well as the symbol of ***Unity,*** whereby it is ***Ahimsa***-that can be the only means to reach ***Truth*** or to recognize ***Him***.

As ***Ahimsa*** is the only means to reach ***Truth***, ***Ahimsa*** being one of two sides of a coin, of which ***Truth*** is the other side, is equal to ***Truth***; therefore, its role in the practices of all walks of human life becomes most important. Mahatma Gandhi stated:

"My love for non-violence is superior to that for every other thing-mundane or supramundane. It is equaled only by love for Truth, which is to me synonymous with non-violence; through which and which alone I can see and reach Truth."

And that is why; Gandhian philosophy or Gandhism, which is an amalgam of Mahatma Gandhi's views and practices, revolves around ***Ahimsa*** [non-violence].

Non-Violence [*Ahimsa*]

Generally, we attribute ***Ahimsa*** [non-violence] as a dictum that prescribes non-snatching of anyone's life. Or in other and simple words, it is said that to refrain from taking the life of any of the living beings is non-violence. But, in reality, this is neither a true meaning of ***Ahimsa*** [non-violence], nor it is a complete derivation pertaining to the concept of it. As ***Ahimsa*** [non-violence] is the state opposite to ***Himsa*** [violence], we can say:

"Total non-violence consists in not hurting some other one's intellect, speech or action by own thought, utterance or deeds and not to deprive some one of his life."[3]

Or in fewer words, we can describe ***Ahimsa*** as follows:

"Abstinence in toto from violence is non-violence."[4]

Mahatma Gandhi, agreeing with this definition of non-violence and connecting it to courage, declared ***Ahimsa*** to be a [continuously] active force.[5] Mahatma Gandhi did not believe ***Ahimsa*** to be a rough thing, an abstract thought or inactive value established by man. He was of the firm belief that ***Ahimsa*** is a dynamic and live value and an essential condition for existence, development and the ultimate goal [even the Unity]. Along with this, non-violence is the strongest force, one to be used properly and wielded with high wisdom, and not with equal ease. In Mahatma Gandhi's own words:

"Ahimsa cannot be dismissed as lightly as you think. Ahimsa is the strongest force known. But if all can use the strongest force with equal ease, it would lose its importance. We have not been able yet to discover the true measure of the innumerable properties of an article of our daily use like water. Some of its properties fill us with wonder. Let us not, therefore, make light of the strongest force like Ahimsa, and let's try to discover its hidden power with patience and faith."[6]

There are some important standards to be noted regarding Gandhian non-violence, especially while inviting the youth of the day to be familiar with it; and the first of them is humility. Humility, ***Vinamrata*** in Indian terms, is the quality of a man free from ego and pride. As there is no place for ego and pride in ***Ahimsa*** [non-violence], it is necessary for a person who claims to be non-violent to practice humility in his daily routines. In this context Mahatma Gandhi said:

"If one has pride and egoism, he is not non-violent. Non-violence is impossible without humility."[7]

Secondly, without self-purification in all segments of life the realization of ***Ahimsa*** as an active force remains a dream only; and in such a situation, how can there be a guarantee of its success? However, in its active form ***Ahimsa*** travels extraordinarily, and then it becomes a miracle. That is why; in declaring non-violence to be an active force and a live value, Mahatma Gandhi called upon self-purification, not just in one or two walks of individual life, and not on some occasions only, but continuously in all walks of life so that it could be fully realized. By such a comprehensive, all-sweeping practice of self-purification and, therefore, of ***Ahimsa***, ***Satya*** [truth] can prevail all-around and the way to unity can be possible. To quote Mahatma Gandhi:

"Identification with everything that lives is impossible without self-purification; without self-purification the observance of the law of Ahimsa must remain an empty dream; God can never be realized by one who is not pure of heart. Self-purification, therefore, must mean purification in all walks of life. And purification being highly infectious, purification of oneself necessarily leads to purification of one's surroundings."[8]

Mahatma Gandhi's emphasis on self-purification may seem to people, especially the young, to be difficult or burdensome. Self-purification may seem possible only for a few, or it may sometimes seem impractical for one reason or another. But for those who are bent upon following the path of ***Ahimsa***, it is not only important but essential.

For the path of ***Ahimsa*** is not an easy one. It is for the brave and not for a coward; it is for sacrifice and not for empty gains.[9] As Mahatma Gandhi stated:

"The path of self-purification is hard and steep. To attain to perfect purity one has to become absolutely passion free in thought, speech and action; to rise above the opposing currents of love and hatred, attachment and repulsion."[10]

Having stated that, Gandhi also admitted:

"I know that I have not in me as yet that triple purity, in spite of constant ceaseless striving for it. That is why; the world's praise fails to move me; indeed it very often stings me. To conquer the subtle passion seems to be harder for than the physical conquest to the world by the force of arms. Ever since my return to India,[11] ***I have had experiences of the dormant passions lying hidden within me. The knowledge of them has made me feel humiliated though not defeated. The experiences and experiments have sustained me and given me great joy. But I know that I have still before me a difficult path to traverse. I must reduce myself to zero. So long as a man does not of his own free will put himself last among his fellow creatures, there is no salvation for him. Ahimsa is the farthest limit of humility."***[12]

Although ***Ahimsa*** occupies its due or supreme place in the ideas and behaviours of atheists or those who do not believe in the power of ***God***-the Supreme Being[13], for Mahatma Gandhi, the source of ***Ahimsa*** is ***God Himself***; for, ***"non-violence succeeds only when we have a real living faith in [Him] God."***[14] It is necessary because Gandhi's philosophy of ***'Unity of Human Life'*** is a synthetic whole, by which ***Ahimsa*** is the means, and it can only be significant if it accepts the existence of ***God*** and makes ***Him*** the basis of that Unity.

Application to Current Conflicts

Now, after becoming familiar with the blueprint of Mahatma Gandhi's philosophy, in which *Ahimsa* is the nucleus, we have to discuss its application to current conflicts. Historically, conflicts, though temporary in nature and subject to transformation by cooperation, are inevitable in various walks of human life including the international field. *Ahimsa* [non-violence], a value permanently present in human nature, in its different forms and through its many supplementary values, shows the way to not only overcome conflicts, but transforms conflicts into cooperation.

Everything in the world is subject to constant change, and conflicts are not exception. The nature of conflict too changes from time-to-time. But no matter if conflicts are inevitable or if the base or root cause of them seems to be the same, Gandhian non-violence accords solution to all problems; it is capable of transforming conflicts into cooperation to make life peaceful and developing, if it is applied according to the demand of time and prevailing circumstances in space.

For example, after passing through the process of development for thousands of years since man's inception[15] on Earth, we are now witnessing the days of globalization. Citizens of the world are continuously coming close to one another in different ways, and in all walks of human life; day-by-day the tempo of mutual cooperation is increasing. Even at the international level, dependence on each other is increasing so much that no nation, no matter how mighty or resourceful it may be, can dream of its development by remaining indifferent and isolated. Today, no nation can remain without being the least affected by any change or series of events occurring at the global level.

In such an unprecedented situation, and I must admit benevolent too, problems or conflicts in all walks of life at all levels in general and at the international level in particular affect and involve more and more people, and for this reason the solution or transformation of them demands collective efforts. In other words, I can say that now we have to march forward together, especially to resolve international problems or transform global conflicts.

The days have gone when a particular group of people or inhabitants of a country indulged in false vanity regarding their historical or geographical superiority. It is time now to face and remove all complications by accepting the situation as it warrants. It is necessary to strengthen globalization alongside the spirit of nationalism. A mature international understanding is most essential; development in mutual cooperation is the need of the hour. But how can we succeed in this regard within the scope of Gandhian philosophy, or in other words, within the domain of ***Ahimsa*** [non-violence]? It is an important question, especially in a completely changed global situation

For the development of such a mature understanding or creating an atmosphere surcharged with cooperation, the only way as per the expectation [of Gandhian philosophy] is the application of non-violent activities to resolve dispute and conflicts. But, they too should be adopted by making them befitting in accordance with the prevailing conditions. Only then concrete results would be feasible. Furthermore, to make them fully practical in international sphere, it is absolutely necessary for parties involved in dispute or a particular conflict that they come forward on the basis of following three fundamental points:

- To be serious;
- To accept reality; and
- To be ready to make sacrifices

Today, as all of us know, there are a number of problems at the international level, some of which are of a very serious nature and have been in existence for decades. I do not want to catalogue them here, but we are all aware that they, from time-to-time, give birth to conflicts. Consequently they not only affect the parties directly involved, but they more or less affect other nations also, making solutions to these conflicts seemingly very difficult, if not impossible. But if the three above-mentioned points are honestly kept in mind by the involved parties during the resolution of a problem and/or transformation of conflict, in my opinion, there should be no doubt of success. But for success to occur, the involved parties must possess great courage, high morality and mature understanding, for which the philosophy of Mahatma Gandhi and his ***Ahimsa*** [non-violence] calls upon the whole world.

For years India, the Motherland of Gandhi, had a dispute with her neighbour Bangladesh regarding the issue of sharing water from the Ganges River. The Ganges mostly flows through India and finally merges in the Bay of Bengal [Indian Ocean] via today's Bangladesh, which was previously a part of India herself. In the seventies India installed the Farakka Barrage on the Ganges, a river management project, which became a matter of serious concern for Bangladesh.[16] But it was during the dialogue processes, the centre of which were the above three points, that these two countries were able to go to the root of the problem, understood each other's difficulties and ultimately entered into a compromise. Although India had to sacrifice a bit more in comparison to Bangladesh, the situation was win-win for both of them. It was definitely the Gandhian way to settle a dispute, and the same process could be feasible to resolve other problems also.

Human history is full of instances relating to conflicts or wars between groups and nations. We have especially before us the example of the two World Wars fought in the Twentieth Century. The First World War [1914-1918] claimed the lives of more than ten million people and severely injured twenty-two and a half million.[17] Similarly, in the Second World War [1939-1945] fifty million people were killed and approximately thirty-five million people were either badly injured or maimed.[18] Most of the countries involved in the two World Wars took between ten and fifteen years respectively to pave the way back to their own re-development[19] and stand again on their own feet. Furthermore, the warring nations, tired of wars and the naked dance of violence and death, aspired for peace and pacifistic measures. For this purpose they formed the League of Nations after the First World War and the United Nations Organization after the Second World War.

But even after formation of them, as evident from the series of events of post war period, many times during the course of dialogue, negotiations, compromises and treaties to transform conflicts or to stop wars, parties concerned did not come forward seriously. They, knowingly or unknowingly, had not been ready to accept the realities, and they had also not come forward to make sacrifices. Instead of honesty and sincerity, diplomacies in their full swing had been there in dialogues, negotiations, compromises and treaties. Resultantly, if they prepared ground for the Second World War in 1918 itself, they also paved the way to a new international situation after the Second World War in 1945, of which the ***Cold War*** and the ***Balance of Power*** were some of the results. Along with this, some other new conflicts emerged, the transformation of which has not been possible to this day.

The Gandhian way is very simple through sincerity, sacrifice, high morality and courage-all essential elements of active ***Ahimsa*** [non-violence]. But it is unfortunate that through the ages we have been habitually reluctant in following a simple pathway such as this. We have accepted that is highly-exaggerated. Even today what I am emphasizing here may not be acceptable to many; it is possible that my views fail to attract the attention of some of you only because I am expressing them in quite a simple way. I am a student of political science. I have studied all aspects of politics, especially relating to international politics including diplomacy. Therefore, I could express my views even on this subject related to Gandhian philosophy and its application to current international conflicts in that manner. But it would not be fair.

The fair thing is that we seriously think over the way shown by Mahatma Gandhi, whose life is like an open book, whose message is simple and straightforward; but for this, we need a high degree of courage, morality and sincerity. And if we could do so, I have no doubt we would overcome all problems, resolve disputes, transform conflicts and pave the way to unity of human life, which is the essence of Gandhian philosophy.

References:

1. An Autobiography or The Story of My Experiments With Truth, page 383
2. Ibid [In this connection Gandhi has written to the extent in his autobiography, ***"My uniform experience has convinced me that there is no other God than Truth. After all, however sincere my striving after Ahimsa may have been, they have still been imperfect and inadequate. The little fleeting glimpses, therefore, that I have been able to have of Truth can hardly convey an idea of the indescrible luster of Truth, a million times more intense than that of sun we daily see with our eyes. In fact what I have caught is only the faintest glimmer of that mighty effulgence. But, this much I can say with assurance, as a result of all my experiments, that a perfect vision of Truth can only follow a complete realization of Ahimsa."*** He also pointed out, ***"Identification with everything that lives is impossible without self purification; without self purification the observance of the law of Ahimsa must remain an empty dream; God can never be realized by one who is not pure by heart. Self purification therefore must mean purification in all the walks of life. And purification being highly infectious, purification of oneself necessarily leads to purification of one's surroundings."***]
3. Gandhian Thoughts, page 75
4. Ibid
5. In it, as Vinoba Bhave also admits, ***"There must be preparedness for battle."*** Vinoba, Shrimannarayan, page 140 [Further, in this connection he points out, ***"Even if non-violence spread through the world, there would be need for preparedness. Neither violence nor non-violence allows room for a man to earn all at***

one time and to enjoy for the rest of his life. It will always be necessary to keep awake the power of resistance. A life of non-violence means not merely occasional sacrifice but perpetual sacrifice, and not merely sacrifice, but joy in sacrifice."]

6. Mahatma, Volume-5, page 303
7. Ibid
8. An Autobiography or The Story of My Experiments With Truth, page 383
9. Gandhian Thoughts, pp 76-77
10. An Autobiography or The Story of My Experiments With Truth, page 383
11. From South Africa
12. An Autobiography or The Story of My Experiments With Truth, page 383
13. Including Gautama the Buddha and Vardhamana Mahavira
14. Mahatma, Volume-5, page 15
15. It is believed that man started his journey of life from one particular place of Earth some one million years ago.
16. Theory and Practice of Gandhian Non-Violence, page 115
17. Towards Peace and Prosperity, page 119
18. Ibid
19. Ibid

Bibliography:

- Gandhi, MK, An Autobiography or The Story of My Experiments With Truth, Navajivan Publishing House, Ahmedabad [India], 1927
- Gandhi, MK, Harijan Weekly, Published Under the Auspices of Harijan Sewak Sangh [1933-41]; by Navajivan Trust, Ahmedabad [India], Between 1942-48

- Kumar, Ravindra, Gandhian Thoughts: An Overview, Gyan Publishing House, New Delhi [India], 2006
- Kumar, Ravindra, Mahatma Gandhi at the Close of Twentieth Century, Anmol Publications, New Delhi [India], 2004
- Kumar, Ravindra, Theory and Practice of Gandhian Non-Violence, Mittal Publications, New Delhi [India], 2002
- Kumar, Ravindra, Towards Peace and Prosperity, World Peace Movement Trust, Meerut, U. P. [India], 2003
- Tendulkar, DG, Mahatma: Life of Mohandas Karamchand Gandhi, 8 Volumes, VK Jhaveri and DG Tendulkar, Bombay [India], 1951-54

****

3

Application of Gandhism in Conflicts of Democracy

"There is no human institution but has its dangers. The greater the institution, the greater the chances of abuse; democracy is a great institution and, therefore, it is liable to be greatly abused."

-MK Gandhi

Gandhi's Personality

Just as he was simple in his personal life, so Mahatma Gandhi was equally simple regarding his work. His personality was neither complicated nor twisted; his appeal to the people was always direct. That is why; during his lifetime he was neither considered an eminent intellectual in the academic sense of the term, nor was he accepted as a great scholar, thinker and philosopher. However, it is another matter that after his passing away he became a centre of study and research for so many scholars and intellectuals of both the East and the West. Perhaps the largest number of books and papers are being published today on the various aspects of life, works and views of Mahatma Gandhi.

Why is this so? The answer to this question is also very simple. It is because the manner, in which he explained the practicality of ***Ahimsa*** [non-violence], and placed it as an effective weapon for direct action, was unique in itself. Despite existing in different forms in both theory and practice, through the ages ***Ahimsa*** [non-violence] was considered merely a personal virtue or value, particularly one to be practiced by ***Rishis, Saints or Incarnations, or Messengers of God*** in the social and religious spheres. However it was Mahatma Gandhi, who, perhaps for the first time in human history, declared it to be a social virtue or value also, calling upon humanity to cultivate it like the other virtues or values in its daily routines. In his own words:

"Non-violence is not a cloistered virtue confined only to the Rishis and the Cave-dwellers. It is capable of being practiced by the millions, not with full knowledge of all its implication, but because it is the law of our species. It distinguishes man from the brute. But man has not shed the brute in him. He has to strive to do so. This striving applies to the practice of non-violence [in all walks of life including political], and not [merely] to the belief in it."[1]

Furthermore he states:

"Surely society is largely regulated by the expression of non-violence in its mutual dealings. What I ask for is an extension of it on a larger, national and international scale."[2]

Mahatma Gandhi, by giving extension and a new dimension to the concept of ***Ahimsa***, declares that the purest non-violence is epitomized by having a tendency…towards spiritual or physical benefit unto everyone without selfishness and with pure thought after cool and clear deliberations. Hence, he rightly believed:

"The final test as it is violence or non-violence is after all the intent underlying the act."[3]

As the whole world knows, through his political actions, basis of which was ***Ahimsa*** [non-violence], he not only led his compatriots to the door of freedom of their motherland, India, and ensured independence from the centuries old shackles of slavery, he also explained ***Ahimsa***'s meaning and its purpose in a comprehensive and all-welfaristic way.[4] In so doing, Mahatma Gandhi revealed a unique, evergreen and exemplary path by which the citizens of the world could employ to attain freedom and secure justice at all levels, particularly in a democracy.

Conflicts in Democracy

Individual freedom, equality, justice, and the welfare of all are the basic tenets of democracy[5]. It does not matter if those ideals are not a reality in toto for one and all, nor if the majority is the final yardstick to measure the people's concurrence. In my opinion, democracy has come to stay as the best way of governing the people politically.

For democracy, as defined by Abraham Lincoln, ***"is the government of the people, for the people, and by the people."***[6]

Besides the presence of the above-mentioned tenets, there is a greater possibility of peace within a democracy as compared to any other form of political system. In a democracy, people are connected with the system directly and indirectly at every level. A democracy provides maximum opportunity for people to progress and develop; above all, people can decide for themselves the best mode of their welfare. And it is for this reason that today a large portion of the world happens to be under the democratic system of government.

Mahatma Gandhi wished for a stateless democracy fully based upon non-violence. He supported the system of the day on the one hand; and on the other, he expressed the desire to continuously improve that system until it arrived within the domain of non-violence. As democracy is a man-made institution it is always subject to improvement; its development and enhancement is a necessity, not an exception. In Mahatma Gandhi's words:

"There is no human institution but has its dangers. The greater the institution, the greater the chances of abuse;

democracy is a great institution and, therefore, it is liable to be greatly abused."[7]

When the potential of abuse is present within a democracy, the potential for conflicts is also inevitable. Then, how can we get rid of conflicts in a democratic system as per the Gandhian way in which ***Ahimsa*** [non-violence] is the nucleus? In my opinion, we can construct a healthy democracy through the maturity of its own organizations and institutions. If they are matured, democracy will be healthy and the more a democracy is healthy the less are the possibilities of conflicts in it. This is the first thing that can be proclaimed openly.

However, this itself raises the question of how a democratic institution can gain maturity as outlined by Mahatma Gandhi? To find the answer to this fundamental and important question, it is necessary for us to analyze Mahatma Gandhi's views about some basic tenets of democracy, of which representation and public opinion are of utmost importance.

Representation and public opinion both play their important roles in the construction and conduction of a democratic government. That is why; Mahatma Gandhi held his own opinion on them and he expressed it exclusively before the world. Regarding representation he said:

"I hold it to be an utter delusion to believe that a large number of delegates are in any way a help to the better conduct of business, or that it safeguards the principle of democracy. Fifteen hundred delegates, jealous of the interests of the people, broadminded and truthful, would any day be better safeguard for a democracy than six

thousand irresponsible men chosen anyhow. To safeguard democracy the people must have a keen sense of independence, self-respect and their oneness, and should insist on choosing, as their representatives, only such persons as are good and true."[8]

No doubt, the following two concrete points pertaining to representation, along with their importance in the system, are quite clear in the above statement of Mahatma Gandhi:

- Consciousness in people for a democracy and the roles of the representatives within it are absolutely necessary; and
- Full care in choosing representatives for the conduction of the system.

Mahatma Gandhi did not consider the number of delegates as important as representatives who would see to the needs and welfare of the people to the maximum possible extent. It did not matter if the representatives were few in number as long as the people's best interests were the main spirit driving the democracy.

Also, it is a healthy and mature public opinion that controls the state and the government. Hence if the system is to be kept fit, it is only possible through healthy public opinion, the repudiation of which would be quite difficult by the state. In the words of the Mahatma himself:

"A popular state can never act in advance of public opinion; if it goes against it, it will be destroyed."[9]

No democracy can be successful without healthy criticism, for well-informed, balanced and matured critique is the backbone of public life in a democracy. In the absence of critical analysis, there is a dread of losing the real form and feature of democracy. Therefore, there is always a need to make the people conscious and aware; there is the necessity to make the government and its representatives familiarized with what the public wants.

But, in spite of it, if the government does not work in accordance with aspirations of people then those resuscitating it, must be aware of their strength. The state or the government cannot even for a moment exist without the goodwill of public opinion.

How can a healthy and mature public opinion be cultivated? According to Mahatma Gandhi it is possible only through the right education. In his emphasis of right and true education, Mahatma Gandhi pointed out that if proper education is not imparted, public opinion can flow in reverse order. And in such a situation it would be very difficult to tolerate it. To quote Mahatma Gandhi himself:

"Healthy public opinion has an influence, of which we have not realized the full significance...Public opinion becomes intolerable when it becomes violent and aggressive."[10]

Majority and Legislation

The principle of the majority plays the key role in a democratic form of government, for the scale of a democracy's establishment is the majority's decision. In such a situation, should whatever the majority decides be accepted? Mahatma Gandhi said that to an extent the decision of the majority should surely be taken for granted; that one should yield to the majority in matters of detail.

However, there is no place for autocracy in democracy, even if the party is in the absolute majority. Individual freedom of each and everyone must be cautiously protected in a democracy. In the case that individual freedom is not protected or it is violated then Mahatma Gandhi held:

"Minority has a perfect right to act differently from the majority."[11]

In spite of the principle of majority as applied within a democracy, Mahatma Gandhi desired the cooperation of both the majority and the minority to establish an ideal society completely free from exploitation. To this end he suggested:

"Let us not push the mandate theory to ridiculous extreme and become slaves to resolution of majorities. That would be a revival of brute force in a more virulent form. If rights of minorities are to be respected, the majority must tolerate and respect their opinion and action...It will be the duty of the majority to see that the minorities receive a proper hearing and are not otherwise exposed to insult."[12]

Mahatma Gandhi also suggested:

"Claiming the right of free opinion and free action as we do, we must extend the same to others. The rule of majority, when it becomes coercive, is as intolerant as that of a bureaucratic minority. We must patiently try to bring round the minority to our view by gentle persuasion and argument."[13]

As Mahatma Gandhi suggested, it is therefore necessary that legislation be patiently deliberated upon before it can be put into practice.

Rights and Duties

Equal rights to all are expected in a democracy. In the absence of them there can be no enjoyment of freedom. According to the Mahatma, if freedom is the interdependence of political, economic and moral spheres,[14] and it is to be shared equally by all without discrimination, including those who are physically weak, e.g., the lame and the helpless, they must be able to contribute equally to its maintenance.

At the same time, in order to acquire rights, everyone is supposed to perform his/her duties. This is why; Mahatma Gandhi stated that the true source of a right is duty. To say, if someone discharges his duties, rights are not far from him. The Mahatma also pointed out that if someone neglecting his duties runs after rights, those rights will escape him like a will of the wisp; the more he pursues them, the further they will fly. In Gandhi's own words:

"If instead of insisting on rights everyone does his duty, there will immediately be the rule of order established among mankind."[15]

Furthermore Mahatma Gandhi believed:

"Rights that do not flow directly from duty well performed are not worth having."[16]

Equality is placed at the highest state in a democracy and individual rights are not the exception. If there are no equal rights for each and everyone, there is no possibility of proportionate progress; it is well-known that in such a state, no democracy can survive for very long. Hence, before having a desire to acquire rights, everyone should be ready to perform his/her duties. It is the best way to strengthen the edifice of democracy as well as the best way to run it on the path of ***Ahimsa*** [non-violence] as outlined by Mahatma Gandhi.

Justice and Punishment

As a manmade institution, democracy cannot be free from conflicts, therefore, how can it be free from crimes? An individual commits small or bigger crimes, no matter if generally this term is used for a legal crime.[17]

If there is a crime, and if it is established, there should definitely be a provision of punishment for it. But how much and what type of punishment should be meted out in a democracy to accord justice for all concerned? In this respect Mahatma Gandhi held his own different views, the root of which can be found in his commitment to non-violence per his following comment regarding redemption:

"I do not seek redemption from the consequences of my sin; I seek to be redeemed from sin itself or rather from the very thought of sin. Until I have attained that end, I shall be content to be restless."[18]

No doubt, a human being commits sin intentionally and unintentionally as the dealings of the world are such that it is impossible for a human being to be wholly rid of sin. If so, then certainly one has to bear the consequences of sin. Hence for the commission of a crime, the provision for punishment is utmost essential. However, the punishment must be of such a nature that it could accord an opportunity for a wrongdoer to reform and amend his/her ways in the future. This is fully within the scope of Gandhian philosophy as well as a step towards making democratic institutions mature and healthy, ultimately strengthening the democracy.

Mahatma Gandhi was of the firm opinion that as the possibility of reform and improvement exists within every human being, he/she must not be deprived of reforming and improving him/herself. That is why; he was in support of abolishing capital punishment altogether.[19]

Conclusion

Now, the conclusion we draw from the above analysis is that democracy, which like other walks of human life is not free of potential of abuses, does not matter if they are temporary, smaller or bigger in nature, can be made free of weaknesses through the maturity and health of its organizations and institutions. In this regard the utmost need is to awaken the masses and make the system responsible in practice as much as possible. Furthermore, there must be all possibilities and provisions for reforms at all levels.

For reforms are the signs of development. An institution such as democracy depends on reforms to achieve its goals to the maximum possible extent because its responsibilities are far greater than any other political institution. Hence, Mahatma Gandhi's simple suggestions to make different democratic organizations mature and healthy are worth contemplating; through his ideas there are all possibilities for democracy's growth and strength. And without a doubt, a deep-rooted and strong democracy can grant considerable relief from conflict and accord well-being for its entire people.

References:

1. Mahatma, Volume-5, page 189
2. Ibid, page 12
3. Young India, 4 October 1928
4. Mahatma, Volume-5, page 267 [Explaining his point of view pertaining to non-violent action in a comprehensive manner, Mahatma Gandhi says, ***"Non-violent action means mobilization of the world opinion in our favour. I know that a growing number of thinking men and women of the world are sick of the war spirit, they are longing for a way of peace, and they are looking to India to tom point that way. We cannot have the opinion on our side if we are not honestly non-violent. And let me repeat what I have said...that I shall be able to fight with a very small army of honest Satyagrahis and shall feel powerless and embarrassed if I have a huge army, in which I can have no trust or as to whose behaviour I am not always sure."***]
5. Collected Essays, page 39
6. Theory and Practice of Gandhian Non-violence, page, 95
7. Young India, 7 May 1931 [Considering Mahatma Gandhi's views pertaining to democracy to be important and significant even today, I am including the full text of his write up, which he contributed for Young India on the 7th May 1931 under the title ***Dangers of Democracy*** as appendix-1 of this manuscript.]
8. An Autobiography or The Story of My Experiments With Truth, page 369
9. Harijan, 13 November 1937
10. Young India, 7 May 1931
11. Theory and Practice of Gandhian Non-violence, page, 103
12. Young India, 8 December 1921
13. Ibid, 26 January 1922

14. Mahatma, Volume-8, page 105
15. Harijan, 6 July 1947
16. Ibid
17. In fact, several times, this term is used for a moral crime also. If anybody indulges in an act that is morally wrong, it will definitely be a crime in moral sense, which in view of the Mahatma, is in no way less than the crime of any other nature.
18. An Autobiography or The Story of My Experiments With Truth, page 90
19. Theory and Practice of Gandhian Non-violence, page, 106

Bibliography:

- Evangelista, Susan, Non-violence: A Text, ISP, Ateneo De Manila University, CC, Manila [The Philippines], 1994
- Gandhi, MK, An Autobiography or The Story of My Experiments With Truth, Navajivan Publishing House, Ahmedabad [India], 1927
- Gandhi, MK, Harijan Weekly, Published Under the Auspices of Harijan Sewak Sangh [1933-41]; by Navajivan Trust, Ahmedabad [India], Between 1942-48
- Gandhi, MK, Sarvodaya, Navajivan Publishing House, Ahmedabad [India], 1955
- Gandhi, MK, Young India Weekly [1919-1931], Reprinted in 13 Volumes by Navajivan Publishing House, Ahmedabad [India], 1984
- Guha, AC, India's Struggle Quarter of a Century, Volume I & II, The Publications Division, Ministry of Information and Broadcasting, Government of India, New Delhi [India], 1982
- Kumar, Ravindra, Champaran to Quit India Movement, Mittal Publications, New Delhi [India], 2002
- Kumar, Ravindra, Collected Essays: Voice of An Indologist, Sara Publications, Meerut [India], 1996

- Kumar, Ravindra, Gandhian Thought: An Overview, Gyan Publishing House, New Delhi [India], 2006
- Kumar, Ravindra, Global Peace-An International Journal of Philosophy, Peace, Education, Culture and Civilization, Volume-1, Number-1 to Volume-6, Number-4, World Peace Movement Trust, Meerut [India], 2001-06
- Kumar, Ravindra, Theory and Practice of Gandhian Non-Violence, Mittal Publications, New Delhi [India], 2002
- Tendulkar, DG, Mahatma: Life of Mohandas Karamchand Gandhi, 8 Volumes, VK Jhaveri and DG Tendulkar, Bombay [India], 1951-54

****

4

Mahatma Gandhi, Gandhism and Culture of Peace

"A curriculum of religious instructions should include a study of the tenets of faiths other than one's own. For this purpose the students should be trained to cultivate the habit of understanding and appreciating the doctrine of various great religions of the world in a spirit of reverence and broad minded tolerance."

-MK Gandhi

Mahatma Gandhi and His Legacy

Mahatma Gandhi was quite a simple man in his personal life. His simplicity can be examined through the following words of Albert Einstein, who was his own contemporary as well as a great scientist of the Twentieth Century:

"Generations to come...will scarcely believe that such a one as this even in flesh and blood walked upon this earth."[1]

Simultaneous to this, the unique legacy and exemplary ideas that Mahatma Gandhi left to humanity were summarized by Einstein as follows:

"Mahatma Gandhi's life achievement stands unique in political history. He has invented a completely new and humane means for the liberation war of an oppressed country, and practiced it with greatest energy and devotion. The moral influence he had on the consciously thinking human being of the entire civilized world will probably be much more lasting than it seems in our time with its overestimation of brutal violent forces. Because lasting will only is the work of such statesmen who wake up and strengthen the moral power of their people through their example and educational works.

"We may all be happy and grateful that destiny gifted us with such an enlightened contemporary, a role model for the generations to come."

Furthermore, Romain Rolland, another great man of the same Century said:

"Mahatma Gandhi is another Christ."[2]

No doubt, the statements of both these great men are extraordinary as they exhort the world to examine Mahatma Gandhi's personality and works as well as their relevance in these times, especially in the context of a development of a culture of peace that can ensure safe existence of mankind as well as the progress and prosperity of all.

Gandhism

Now, prior to analyzing the importance and significance of views and works of Mahatma Gandhi in the context of the development of a culture of peace, it is necessary for us to know what his ideas are, or in other words, what Gandhism is.

Mahatma Gandhi himself was extremely opposed to bringing his philosophy or ideas under the domain of any ***'ISM'***. For to him, setting his ideas with ***'ISM'*** meant to flee from the spirit behind them and to minimize their importance. But even so, his ideas are generally known as Gandhism, and, in reality, this is not the true introduction of Gandhism, because Gandhism does not merely consist of the ideas, which he put forth before the world. In Gandhism also includes what he treated in his individual life in accordance with these ideas to the maximum possible extent. Those who hold merely his theory or ideas to be Gandhism are incorrect, because his ideas alone cannot be accepted as Gandhism.

As known to the whole world, Gandhism revolves around ***Ahimsa*** [non-violence][3], which is the most ancient, perpetual, individual as well as social, all timely and welfaristic value; it is an active force, connected with God and, thus, stays to be true, and it is a ***Dharma*** in grandeur.[4] Along with this, non-violence is permanently present in human nature, and it is an essential condition for existence; moreover, it is the basis of human development and the means to achieve the goal.

We can all well understand our will to live. We can wish eagerly for our development. But what is the goal of life? Sometimes we do not understand it. In fact, from both the spiritual and social point of view, peace is the goal of life. It is the purpose behind the creation[5] for almost everyone, whether he is atheist or theist. And it is because of this that emphasis has been laid on the continuing awakening and adoption of non-violence, individually and collectively, in our day-to-day practices.

Not only by ***Tirthankara*** Mahavira, in whom manifestation of ***Ahimsa*** [non-violence] took place in the best possible manner[6], or the Buddha and Mahatma Gandhi[7], but also by other apostles of peace, philosophers and thinkers of both, the East and the West, efforts were made for the construction of a culture accepting non-violence to be the fundamental or nucleus so that the existence of mankind is assured, the path of development is smoothened and the ultimate goal is well within sight and approach. There is no let-up in these endeavours; and this process shall continue with the same gusto in future as well.

The history of mankind, which measures billions of years and is divided into different ages, has proven time and again the fact that among all other beings, only man possesses the qualities of intellect and creativity. It is due to this that he has been able to pass through the process of learning by doing. In other words, especially from a Gandhian point of view, this is the real education, which played a very vital role and made a sizeable contribution to the awakening of non-violence and its application in daily practices, regardless of the method adopted with the changing times. It was necessary from the point of view of those who define education as ***"Sa Vidyaya Vimuktey."***[8]

As the whole world knows, in this very chain, in the Twentieth Century, Mahatma Gandhi made a momentous contribution by showing a wonderful, simple and justifiable way of awakening and practicing of non-violence in the routine chores of life. The reason behind accepting the above way of Mahatma Gandhi to be wonderful, simple and justifiable is that he, by establishing co-ordination and synthesis amongst all concepts of the East and the West, old and new, makes non-violence well worthy to be grasped by all. Everyone can, more or less, find non-violence of his imagination in Gandhi's principle pertaining to it, and can also adopt it in his practices. It is only the great characteristic of his non-violence and due to this it is unique as also of special recognition. In this regard once more I would like to quote Albert Einstein who says:

"I believe that Gandhi's views were the most enlightened of all the political men in our time."

Gandhi, Education and Culture of Peace

To make non-violence the basis of maximum day-to-day practices of man, Mahatma Gandhi considered it to be an indivisible, important and essential part of education. The development of morality and ethics in man beginning in childhood, i.e. by imparting moral and ethical education from the onset of his primary studies and beyond, is the most important step in this regard. This is an essential part of the fourfold[9] educational plans, which I have proposed, one that is necessary for all-around development of personality in general, and the pathway to peace in particular. Also, it is one of the two aspects[10] of Mahatma Gandhi's unique and refined approach pertaining to value education, which provides us with a new dimension of development in the matter. Through this, Mahatma Gandhi believed that education of intellect in the true sense would emerge. In the words of the Mahatma:

"Education means all-round drawing out of the best in child [student] **and *man-body, mind and spirit."***[11]

By Mahatma Gandhi's imagination and definition, education incorporates proper exercise and the training of the bodily organs, i.e. hands, feet, eyes, ears, nose, etc; this provides the best and quickest way of developing morality and ethics, without which the awakening of the soul is not possible. If this is not so, it has no worth; it is incomplete and aimless.

It is a fact that an education system that lacks morality and ethics cannot be termed as good and complete in its term and objective. The reason behind this is that a student or man who lacks morals and ethics cannot be considered healthy in the mental and physical sense, as self-control and good character are essential for health. In the absence of morality and ethics, no one can differentiate between right and wrong and in such a state, all-round development of his personality[12] is impossible.

A person who is not a moralist and does not differentiate between right and wrong cannot rise to the essential level of the true student. And the one, who does not rise to this level, surely cannot contribute towards the development of a culture of peace. In the words of Mahatma Gandhi:

"Through education all-round development...can take place only when it proceeds with the education of the physical and spiritual [that essentially includes moral or ethical knowledge] faculties of the child."[13]

For the construction of a culture of peace, the attainment of spiritual growth that Mahatma Gandhi believed is an essential part of education can be attained only through morality and ethics. Seeing this from another perspective also yields the same point, when we consider education as a means of attaining salvation-***Sa Vidyaya Vimuktey***-as well as a support on the pathway to complete peace and liberation, we cannot differentiate it from spiritualism.

It is for this reason that the Mahatma laid down policies to ensure that morality and righteousness would always be considered an essential and requisite part of a student's education, thereby guaranteeing they would reap the benefits of knowledge and spirituality.

Mahatma Gandhi was of the firm opinion that students should be educated under the strict regimen of high morals, self-control and right thinking; he also believed that they provide service to society by following tradition with a constant awareness of their duties. These responsibilities include respect towards one's elders, e.g. parents, teachers and other authority figures, and as well as a loving and dependable conscientiousness for those younger than oneself. After all, it is both duties and responsibilities that are important and significant not just in maintaining peace, but in building a sound culture of peace.

Religious Education and Peace

Mahatma Gandhi was in favour of religious education to be imparted to students in schools and colleges. On the 25th of August, 1927 he wrote in Young India:

"I know...that a country like India, where there are most religions of the world represented and where there are so many denominations in the same religion, there must be difficulty about making provision for religious instruction. But if India is not to declare spiritual bankruptcy, religious instruction of its youth must be held to be at least as necessary as secular instruction."

The words ***"at least as necessary as secular instruction"*** are of utmost importance as they clearly state Mahatma Gandhi's views. For the Mahatma rightly believed that many fundamental beliefs are shared in the teachings of the world's religious communities. All faiths, he asserted, equally emphasize morality, love to others, ethics and other righteous qualities that lead a human being to contribute to peace in society.

Thus, the purpose behind Mahatma Gandhi's advocacy of the introduction of religious studies in education was his intention to strengthen students' morality and ethics. This kind of education instills the values of forbearance, tolerance, and reverence in one's character. And in turn, these values are supplementary and fully within the domain of the great and perpetual value ***Ahimsa*** [non-violence]. Explaining the importance and need of religious education, Mahatma Gandhi declared in an issue of Young India:

"A curriculum of religious instructions should include a study of the tenets of faiths other than one's own. For this purpose the students should be trained to cultivate the habit of understanding and appreciating the doctrine of various great religions of the world in a spirit of reverence and broad minded tolerance."[14]

To guarantee that moral and ethical education is imparted to students, and ensure that it has a permanent place in a person's life, Mahatma Gandhi placed the responsibility of this goal upon all members of society-be they parents, teachers, the leaders of the society, or the student himself. However, he especially called upon all teachers to pass on the proper knowledge of morality and ethics to students at the primary, secondary and higher level of education. To quote Mahatma Gandhi:

"This if properly done would [definitely] ***help to give them a spiritual assurance*** [to pave way to a culture of peace] ***and also to a better appreciation..."***[15]

By suggesting guidelines for teachers, Gandhi asserted that it is the duty of teachers to develop the high morals and strong character of their students. If teachers fail to do so, it means they fall short of their social and national responsibilities and as such, they are insincere towards their noble profession. He also said that a teacher should set an example for students and society to follow. This can only be done when a teacher himself leads life with high standards of morality and strong character. An ideal teacher should be free from any addiction. He needs to be polite and should set an ideal example of simple living and high thinking. He should also remember that wasting time is a sin; therefore, he should be mindful of his duties towards students and society. Moreover, he should have a good reputation in society from a moral and ethical point of view.

Mahatma Gandhi also called upon the students to remember that it should be their foremost duty to make certain that moral and ethical knowledge continues to be the integral part of their educational process. By doing so, students contribute to the development of value education that is so essential for the formation of an ideal, peaceful and prosperous society. Furthermore, the Mahatma strongly encouraged the pursuit of moral and ethical knowledge even after formal education is completed, calling upon each and everyone to seek it till the last breath of life.

Value Education and Culture of Peace

The other aspect of the Gandhian approach as it relates to value education is also important for the construction of a sustainable culture of peace. This aspect deals with basic or technical education, does not matter if the word ***'Buniyadi'*** was used by Mahatma Gandhi in the third and the fourth decades of the Twentieth Century, meaning the knowledge or education that could help people promote handicrafts and establish cottage industries in India.

The ultimate purpose behind Mahatma Gandhi's ideas was to assist young men and women to become self-reliant in the economic field. From a present-day perspective, his ideas pertaining to ***Buniyadi*** [basic] education are still worthy and considerable. For Gandhi's initiatives have no conflict with the concept of today's job-oriented or technical education; they can make a man self-dependent and prosperous. And it is without a doubt that a self-reliant and prosperous person contributes towards the prosperity of a society and nation, as well as a stable and real culture of peace.

The importance and significance of the Gandhian approach multiplies as he emphasized the imparting of technical knowledge from the very beginning of study based upon the careful identification of that predominant virtue from amongst those virtues, which every child possesses.

In today's completely changed circumstances, I believe there may not be another sound alternative to it. I also believe that if people around the world study this approach carefully, it can be applicable everywhere according to the prevailing circumstances and can definitely yield good results.

Conclusion

This is what Mahatma Gandhi accomplished so that every human being on this planet could live without fear, assured of a safe and secured life, marching equally towards a development process, possessing peace while strengthening the culture of peace.

Gandhism and its system of education, especially pertaining to value education, is ultimately the education of a peace whose purpose is to make a man fully developed. This, according to Mahatma Gandhi is:

"An unending process divided into different stages…"

The worth of it lies in the idea that education's foundations should be laid on sound morals and ethics and should by necessity enable a man to be self-dependent.

It is undoubtedly ever-relevant in achieving the goal of peace and for the construction of a real and sustainable culture of peace, especially under the democratic system of government. In this context its relevance and importance can never be underestimated; and it should be applied on the grander scale. The need of the day is to study, understand and adopt the Gandhian approach to the education process, putting it into practice all over the world. Indeed it is the demand of the times.

References:

1. Gandhian Thoughts: An Overviews, page 15
2. Ibid, page 123
3. Although abstinence in toto from violence is non-violence; or non-violence consists in not hurting some other one's thought, utterance and deeds by one's own thought, utterance and deeds, and not to deprive a living being of his life, but regarding the acid test, necessary for non-violence, Mahatma Gandhi's argument ***'that the ultimate yardstick of violence and non-violence is the intention behind the action'***, deserves due consideration.
4. In all of its meaning whether adoption of good, or duty or the way of life.
5. In case we accept the view that there is no purpose behind creation [of human being], our life become simply meaningless. That's why; we must accept the idea of purposefulness, does not matter if we are atheists or theists. Be it the Buddha or ***Tirthankara***

Mahavira, Lord Jesus Christ or Prophet Muhammad, everyone was of the singular opinion that there was a purpose behind the creation of mankind.

6. Who declares it to be the soul-force
7. Who, ultimately, accepts it to be a natural value
8. Meaning thereby, ***'education makes capable of liberation'***
9. The other three are: General [according to prescribed syllabus], physical and technical [***Buniyadi***]
10. Another one is basic [***Buniyadi*** or technical] education
11. Mahatma Gandhi in the Beginning of Twenty-First Century, page 32
12. About all-round development, Mahatma Gandhi has written in the issue of Harijan on the 31st July, 1937 that in it he wants to draw out of the best in child and man-body, mind and spirit; only literacy is not the end of education or even the beginning.
13. Harijan, 8 May 1937
14. Young India, 6 December 1928 [See appendix-2 for the full text of Mahatma Gandhi's views, which he expressed through a short article published on this subject in Young India on the 6th December 1931 under the title ***Religious Education***]
15. Young India, 6 December 1923

Bibliography:

- Fischer, Louis, Gandhi: His Life and Message for the World, New American Library, New York, [USA], 1954
- Gandhi, MK, Harijan Weekly, Ahmedabad, [India], 15 July 1939; 30 September 1939; 6 July 1940
- Gandhi, MK, Yong India, Weekly, Ahmedabad, [India], 6 December 1923; 4 October 1928
- Green, Martin, Tolstoy and Gandhi, Men of Peace: A Biography, Basic Books, New York, [USA], 1983

- Kumar, Ravindra, Essays on Gandhism and Peace, Krishna Publications, Meerut, [India], 1999
- Kumar, Ravindra, Gandhian Thoughts: An Overview, Gyan Publishing House, New Delhi, [India], 2006
- Kumar, Ravindra, Mahatma Gandhi at the Close of Twentieth Century, Anmol Publications, New Delhi, [India], 2004
- Kumar, Ravindra, Mahatma Gandhi in the Beginning of Twenty-First Century, Gyan Publishing House, New Delhi, [India], 2006
- Kumar, Ravindra, Theory and Practice of Gandhian Non-Violence, Mittal Publications, New Delhi, [India], 2001
- Tendulkar, DG, Mahatma: Life of Mohandas Karamchand Gandhi, Volume-5, VK Jhaveri & DG Tendulkar, Bombay, [India], 1952
- Tolstoy, Leo, The Law of Violence and the Law of Love, The Unicorn Press, London, [U K], 1959

****

5

Relevance of Gandhism for Society and Students

"I have always held that social justice, even to the least and the lowliest is impossible of attainment by force. I have further believed that it is possible by further training of the lowliest by non-violent means to secure redress of the wring suffered by them. That means is non-violent non-cooperation."

-MK Gandhi

General Observation

During his lifetime, Mahatma Gandhi neither wrote any particular book on society nor did he contribute a series of articles to systematically express his views on it; even then, he had a vast understanding of society's foundations and its functioning through its different parts. And it was through that knowledge that he delved to the root of those social problems, particularly those concerning the Indian society, which were most serious in his own time, some of which still exist today. He then offered suggestions to make society healthy, prosperous and free of problems based on equality, fraternity, mutual trust and understanding.

For example, let us examine Mahatma Gandhi's views about class war in India between capitalist and labour or suggestions offered by him addressing the conflict between landlords or Zamindars and farmers. In this context he said:

"Class war is foreign to the essential genius of India, which is capable of evolving Communism broad-based on fundamental rights of all on equal justice."[1]

If we analyze this short statement by Mahatma Gandhi in an Indian context, we find it true to a large extent. In the entire history of India, despite the division of society into more than three thousand and five hundred Castes and Sub-castes, there is not a single instance of class war as imagined and interpreted by the Communists. Composed of composite culture, Indian society is chiefly characterized as never having allowed the seed of class war to germinate even for a time, especially during the last century, despite efforts made in this regard. Also it should be believed that there is no such possibility in the near future.

But it should never be interpreted that Mahatma Gandhi advised the exploited to surrender before exploiters or that he wanted them to bend before injustice. To quote the Mahatma:

"I never said there should be cooperation between the exploiter and the exploited so long as exploitation and the will to exploit persist."[2]

Then what to do? Mahatma Gandhi first went to the root of the problem. In this respect, he said that to believe that capitalists or the Zamindars are all exploiters by inherent necessity or that there is a basic or irreconcilable antagonism between their interests and those of the masses is incorrect. Therefore, to then regard the capitalists or Zamindars to be the masses' permanent enemies is also not correct. In fact, according to Mahatma Gandhi, those who are exploited are their own enemies, for exploitation is based on the cooperation, willing or forced, of the exploited. Hence, there would be no exploitation if the exploited refuses to obey the exploiter. However, this must be done in the non-violent way of Mahatma Gandhi, or through Gandhism, by transformation of the present relationship into something healthier and purer and not with an intention to destroy capitalists and Zamindars.

Mahatma Gandhi had the same approach not just in this particular matter related to capitalists and labour, or Zamindars and farmers, but in all other issues related to society, i.e., to go to the root of the problem first and then to introspect.

When these two things are done without bowing before injustice or surrendering to exploitation, it is expected that the exploited will refuse to cooperation with the exploiter in a humanely manner without having ill-will.

Gandhi on Society and Social Issues

In spite of not writing any books or special series of articles on social issues, as stated already, Mahatma Gandhi was fully aware of them and was very concerned about the problems related to society. That is why; he occasionally expressed his views publicly as well as through the columns of his own weeklies like Young India, Navajivan, Harijan, Harijan-Sewak and other Indian periodicals, and also through the columns of Indian Opinion, which he wrote during his stay in South Africa. It is doubtless to say that on one hand, the basis of all of them was his experiences of life,[3] and on the other it was his thinking or realizations that definitely were subject to change during his own lifetime

For Mahatma Gandhi, society is a structure, in which most of the relations are carried-out on the basis of mutual cooperation. In other words, mutual cooperation is the basis of conduction of day-to-day behaviours of society. The essence that can be drawn from Mahatma Gandhi's opinion is that all are equal in society; consent and cooperation is inevitable to carry-out its activities; and in principle, ***"none amongst members of society is low, none high, even in the individual body, the head is not high because it is the top of the body, nor are the soles of the feet low because they touch the earth."***[4]

And clearly:

"Even as members of the individual body are equal, so are the members of society."[5]

For Mahatma Gandhi, society is the chief ground for transforming the concept of ***'all life is one'*** into reality. It is the same concept, in which he believed the unity of human life is a synthetic whole that can neither be divided nor distinguished by different levels or social, religious, political, moral or ethical spheres. And by ridding society of problems and rendering it free from conflicts, the masses can march forward on the pathway of ***Sarvodaya*** [greatest good for all instead of the great good for the greatest number], where in addition to equality and freedom, there are all possibilities to lead a happy life and social justice to each and everyone is guaranteed.

Gandhi, Society and Social Justice

To accord social justice to all in society without any discrimination was the sole desire of Mahatma Gandhi, and it was in this regard that he worked throughout his public life. He was fully aware of the consequences if social justice was denied at any time to anyone. That is why; he said he always believed that social justice, even to the least and the lowliest, is essential. And it was for this reason that he called upon the people to not cooperate with those who were the enemies of social justice.

But as we know, Mahatma Gandhi's theories and practices of non-cooperation are within the domain of non-violence. He never considered any concrete result if a means outside the scope of non-violence was applied to establish justice. In his own words:

"I have always held that social justice, even to the least and the lowliest is impossible of attainment by force. I have further believed that it is possible by further training of the lowliest by non-violent means to secure redress of the wring suffered by them. That means is non-violent non-cooperation."[6]

Declaring justice and freedom to be most important for life; their establishment to be an individual duty; and the failing of which meaning readiness to accept slavery, Mahatma Gandhi stated:

"No one is bound to cooperate in one's own undoing or slavery. [Similarly] ***freedom received through the effort of others, however benevolent, cannot be retained when such effort is withdrawn."***[7]

To sum up the above pertaining to Mahatma Gandhi's views about society and social issues, we can say that he was fully aware of its existing problems. To root-out those problems, he was for the freedom and the equality of all. Above all he was for social justice, which plays a vital role not only in according freedom and equality to each and everyone but in leading individuals, as well as society as a whole, towards prosperity. The Mahatma was not willing to compromise at the cost of individual freedom, equality and social justice. He appealed to the masses for non-cooperation through the means of non-violence, which to Mahatma Gandhi was not a mere philosophical principle but the rule and energy of his life,[8] while functioning at the same time as the means of his concept regarding the unity of human life.

Gandhi and Students

Considering the role and contribution of educated youths [or students] for society and the nation to be vital, Mahatma Gandhi said:

"My hope lies in you [youth/students of the country]**."**[9]

And:

"[Being] ***the father of tomorrow,*** [you] ***should be the salt of the nation. If the salt loses its flavour wherewith shall it be salted?"***[10]

This is why; he emphasized the constant development of those virtues, which could make the youth mentally, physically, morally and ethically healthy and strong. At the same time, he called upon the young students to maintain strong discipline, to have purity in life, and to adhere to truth while attaining knowledge, as purity and truth are more important in life than mere knowledge alone. To quote the Mahatma:

"Put all your knowledge, learning and scholarship in one scale and truth and purity in the other and the latter will be far outweighing the other."[11]

The Mahatma was concerned over moral impurity, lack of discipline, and wrong acts of students, which he himself witnessed in the 1930s;[12] he also witnessed educated youths, whom, instead of accomplishing their duties towards society and the nation, were engaged in selfish motives, which in his opinion was an act that endangered everyone. Regarding this state of affairs, he laid the responsibility upon all concerned, especially the teaching community, emphasizing the kind of education, which could assure a student's independence while preparing a solid foundation for a student's development.

Mahatma Gandhi was of the firm opinion that a nation intend to pursue the path of true development had to accord equal opportunities and freedom to all its citizens to make certain that each and every citizen on its land participated in its making. Furthermore it must take steps so that everyone without discrimination passes through the process of education with the right direction. For, it is education that can make an individual disciplined, responsible, independent and career-oriented; solving problems at different levels on the one hand, while paving the way to progress on the other.

Education with Right Direction

Education with right direction as imagined by Mahatma Gandhi, which I have spoken about in India and abroad, is a complete educational process comprising of four kinds of learning through which I believe the real objective of education can be achieved. In it, apart from the general education that is imparted according to the syllabus set for the purpose of each different level, there are the provisions of physical, moral and technical learning.

Most schools generally impart two types of education these days: general [according to the prescribed syllabus] and physical education. General education, as we know, ends with the earning of a degree; physical education on the other hand consists of games, sports and different kinds of body-exercises, which are definitely important for both physical and mental development.

In this process, moral education occupies third place. Without a doubt, it helps the student grow into a full-fledged, responsible and duty-bound adult. And if he lacks this education, do you know what the consequences would be? On the basis of general education he will earn a degree; through physical education he will grow strong and will become mentally sound. But in the absence of moral education he will not become a good human being, no matter if he possesses extraordinary virtues. In the absence of proper moral education he will definitely lack even those qualities that are expected from an ordinary human being, such as tolerance, good conduct, willingness to cooperate, love for justice, and obedience.

A number of examples are before us, in which we find many physically strong, mentally developed, handsome and charming persons who occupied the highest political position in their respective countries. But due to lack of moral education, they crossed all limits of general ethics and pushed the whole world to the brink of destruction. I do not need to name any particular person as all of them must be known to us. The series of the two World Wars, especially the Second World War, are before us where we find such people who, due to lack of moral education, have been responsible for the destruction of property and mass killing of innocent people. This will come to pass again even in the present if there is a lack of moral education.

On the contrary, there are also so many instances, which amply prove that from time-to-time morally upright people set the world upon the path of prosperity, succour and peace. They saved humanity even if they were physically infirm, did not look charming or did not hold high degrees of education.

That is why; the importance and significance of moral education cannot be minimized or underestimated. All those concerned with the process of education around the world must understand that if they fall short of properly imparting moral education from the beginning of a child's formal study, it will lead to a weakening of that aspect in his future-life, which otherwise is going to make him morally sound, or a true human being.

In this educational process, the fourth type is technical learning. It is very similar to the Gandhian term, '***Buniyadi***.'[13] Although this does not mean that a student who falls within the domain of this particular learning will fail to appreciate social etiquette, its importance lies in the fact that through technical learning the student will become independent, which according to Gandhi is the prime objective of education.

Now let me clarify my point in a simple manner regarding technical education. We are well aware that almost all of the world's countries, developed, developing, under-developed or poor, are more or less facing the problem of unemployment. A large number of handsome, healthy and qualified youths are jobless. They do not have any work to do and the education they have acquired is of no use to them. Therefore, it is imperative for schools to impart technical knowledge from the very beginning of study in order to get rid of unemployment and to make education meaningful, thereby assuring the all-round development of a student's personality.

Please note, however, that there is a need for doing one's preparation by those who intend to impart this type of education, as there is no place for unnecessary haste as this is not a short-cut method. There is a need to identify that predominant virtue from amongst those virtues, which every child possesses and which may be termed as God-gifted, familial, ancestral, inherited or natural. After this identification, the development of technical knowledge in a child must be predominantly based on that very virtue while imparting the other three types of education to him, which will gradually lead him to a proficiency in the particular trade of technical learning.

On the basis of this learning he will be able to select his future goal while acquiring the middle or secondary level of education. And, thus, with the earning of a degree or equivalent to it, he will not face difficulty in becoming self-dependent because of this technical learning or knowledge. He will have the ability to start his own work independently on the basis of his technical know-how in case he fails to get a job. Therefore, it will also be proper to call it practical training, which helps a student to become self-dependent.

Today it is the duty of all schools to prepare the student to obtain his degree; to work for his physical and mental development; to see that he through moral learning becomes ideal human being; and also to assure his independence by guiding him in the field of technical knowledge pre-dominantly on the basis of the principal virtue, which he always possesses.

Mahatma Gandhi was a practical man. He went to the roots of problems, and through his experiences he drew solutions for them. For society and students he had extraordinary views. He was for the self-stuffiness and all-round development of students. And no one can deny the fact that independent and prosperous students can lead society and the nation in the right direction. So it is high time that the way shown by Mahatma Gandhi be taken seriously and followed with necessary modification as per the demand of time and space.

References:

1. Amrit Bazar Patrika, 2 August 1934
2. Ibid
3. In this regard on the 4th April 1933, Mahatma Gandhi wrote in Harijan, ***"I would like to say to the diligent readers of my writings and to others who are interested in them that I am not at all concerned with appearing to be consistent. In my search after Truth I have discarded many ideas and learnt many new things. Old as I am in age, I have no feeling that I have ceased to grow inwardly or that my growth will stop at the dissolution of the flesh. What I am concerned with is my readiness to obey the call of Truth, my God, from moment-to-moment, and, therefore, when anybody finds any inconsistency between any two writings of mine, if he has still faith in my sanity, he would do well to choose the later of the two on the same subject."***
4. Mahatma Gandhi in his article contributed under the title, ***'Who is a Socialist'*** for Harijan of the 13th July 1947, expressed these views. In this context he further said, ***"In it the prince and the peasant, the wealthy and the poor, the employer and employee are all on the same level."***
5. Harijan, 13 July 1947
6. Harijan, 20 April 1940
7. Ibid

8. Gandhian Philosophy of Non-Violence and ***Satyagraha*** [Quoted from the article by Volodymyr Dick Kyselov, Appeared in the Mahatma Gandhi at the Close of Twentieth Century, page 7]
9. Young India, 9 July 1925
10. Ibid, 22 December 1927
11. Ibid, 21 February 1929
12. Of the Twentieth Century
13. Basic

Bibliography:

- Fischer, Louis, Gandhi: His Life and Message for the World, New American Library, New York [USA], 1954
- Gandhi, MK, An Autobiography or The Story of My Experiments With Truth, Navajivan Publishing House, Ahmedabad [India], 1927
- Gandhi, MK, India of My Dreams, Navajivan Publishing House, Ahmedabad, Gujarat [India], 1957 and Seventh Reprint, 1999
- Gandhi, MK, Harijan Weekly, Published Under the Auspices of Harijan Sewak Sangh [1933-41]; by Navajivan Trust, Ahmedabad [India], Between 1942-48
- Gandhi, MK, Young India Weekly [1919-1931], Reprinted in 13 Volumes by Navajivan Publishing House, Ahmedabad [India], 1984
- Kumar, Ravindra, Education, Culture and Civilization, Krishna Publications, Meerut, Uttar Pradesh [India], 1999
- Kumar, Ravindra, Essays on Gandhism and Peace, Krishna Publications, Meerut, Uttar Pradesh [India], 1999
- Kumar, Ravindra, Gandhi and Gandhism, Part-First, World Peace Movement Trust, Meerut, Uttar Pradesh [India], 2001
- Kumar, Ravindra, Mahatma Gandhi at the Close of Twentieth Century, Anmol Publications Pvt. Ltd. , New Delhi [India], 2004

****

6

Relevance of Gandhi's *Ahimsa* and *Satyagraha* Today

"True love is boundless like the ocean and rising and swelling within one spreads itself out and crossing boundaries and frontiers envelops the whole world."

-MK Gandhi

Introduction

The litmus test of the relevance of works and views of a great man is definitely the application of them in the prevailing conditions of time and space. Mahatma Gandhi is fortunately among those few great men in the entire human history, whose life, works and views [which are also known as Gandhism] have not only proved to be great and exemplary during his own lifetime, but whose relevance and significance has remained intact after his passing away.

For Gandhi became an ideal hero for thousands around the world, particularly renowned figures like Martin Luther King Jr. of America, Nelson Mandela of South Africa, and Ninoy Aquino of the Philippines. At the same time, his views and works are still worth giving a thought, and if they are applied according to the prevailing conditions of time and space, they are no doubt fully capable of bringing sound and beautiful results beyond expectations.

How can this happen? To familiarize ourselves with this attainable reality, it would be appropriate to look at those simple but most humanistic bases, which have been present in Mahatma Gandhi's personal practices and public actions, especially during the National Liberation Movement of India between 1917 and 1942.

Basis of Success during Lifetime

For Mahatma Gandhi, ***Ahimsa*** [non-violence] is a ***Dharma***, no matter if for him it is ***"a plant of slow growth;"***[1]

and along with its activities, which are applicable in daily practices, it is the means to achieve the goal. ***Satyagraha***, pursuit of truth and fully imbibed within ***Ahimsa***, is the weapon he applied in his political actions.

Mahatma Gandhi largely succeeded in ***Ahimsa*** and ***Satyagraha*** because he was brave, humble and free from hatred. All these three are fully within the scope of non-violence; in other words they are themselves the best introduction of ***Ahimsa***. And Mahatma Gandhi practiced them in the best possible manner both in his individual and public life.

Furthermore, he loved everybody without any discrimination. Love is a value supplementary to ***Ahimsa***. It is an ornament of the brave. In it everything is good, positive and beneficial provided it is not momentary. Mahatma Gandhi saw the ultimate Truth in love and said:

"To see the universal and pervading spirit of Truth face-to-face one must be able to love the meanest of creation as myself."[2]

This is why; his non-violence was that of the brave: it was not born out of cowardice.

As for his pure love, he was prepared to suck the poison from the body of General Michael O'Dwyer if he was bitten by a snake. He said:

"True love is boundless like the ocean and rising and swelling within one spreads itself out and crossing boundaries and frontiers envelops the whole world."[3]

This is why; he did not hate the British; it was their exploitative rule he opposed.

Gandhi was free from fear. His fearlessness too was extraordinary and of a very high order. It was during the Champaran ***Satyragraha*** in 1917-1918 when he heard that a British Indigo planter wanted to kill him if he was found alone. Gandhi then went alone to the residence of that planter early one morning and offered him to be killed. The Englishman had no heart to kill this great and brave soul.

In March 1930 the Mahatma, along with selected colleagues, was on his way to Dandi from his Sabarmati ***Ashram***[4] to break the ***Salt Law***, and hence to launch the historical Civil Disobedience Movement. A man from a place near Bharoach, who was opposed to the Gandhian way of ***Ahimsa***, threatened to kill him in a lonely place. The news reached the ears of the Mahatma, the worshipper of non-violence and a fearless and brave soul. He knew that anyone having ill-will cannot withstand the power of non-violence. A few days passed. In the meantime, the Mahatma ascertained the name and address of the person who meant harm, and one day in the early hours, he reached his home and told him:

"Brother! I am Gandhi; you want my life. Take it soon, none will know."[5]

But the man of ill-will could not stand eye-to-eye with the votary of non-violence and he became a follower of the Mahatma. This is the reality of fearlessness and pure love, the basis of which is ***Ahimsa***.

Way of *Satyagraha* in Current Perspectives

The Gandhian approach needs both courage and freedom from ill-will. Before launching ***Satyagraha*** and during the course of ***Satyagraha***, Gandhi was ever ready to negotiate and discuss.

In the late 1920s, Gandhi was opposed to the exploitation of the textile workers of Ahmedabad by the millowners, but he was not fond of a strike to end it.[6] In this regard and all other matters of dispute, whether great or small in nature, local or national, Mahatma Gandhi advocated dialogue, negotiation, reconciliation, arbitration and adjudication as the last resort.

Mahatma Gandhi applied the same method in his actions taken time-to-time for the independence of the country. He inspired confidence and faith in his words; he was always dependable. Even today, in completely changed circumstances it is necessary that when we talk of ***Ahimsa*** [non-violence] and ***Satyagraha***, we should bear this background in our minds.

Today most of the world's countries are facing various kinds of internal and external crises. Due to unprecedented changes in the social, political, economic and cultural spheres, agitations amongst various groups of people have reached the highest level. That is why; particular groups create problems, sometimes of such a serious nature that authorities become helpless. We have witnessed such situations in the provinces of Punjab and Asam, as well as other parts of India during the last two decades of the past century.

In such a state of world affairs, can the way shown by Mahatma Gandhi still be relevant? Can his ***Ahimsa*** and ***Satyagraha*** be applied to tackle such problems? Yes, it is possible. But it is necessary to become familiar with the methods of their application in today's changed circumstances. Both ***Ahimsa*** and ***Satyagraha*** are not the exceptions to the law of change; they too fall within its domain. Therefore, success of them depends upon their application according to demand of time and space.

So those in authority dealing with serious issues in the world must have the humility to understand and accommodate the opposing point of view. They should have love and regard for those who cry for justice and rights, and even those clamouring for separation. In that case there would be room for discussion, negotiation and settlement.

Non-violence and ***Satyagraha*** [pursuit of Truth] presuppose humility and the readiness to understand even the most unpleasant stand of the opponent. This is applicable to those in power if they want to deal with the problem non-violently.

For those who cry for justice and freedom and knowingly or unknowingly under its guise clamour for separation, the non-violent ***Satyagraha*** would mean determined non-cooperation without ill-will, dogged determination to suffer for their rights and the readiness to compromise if their demand is substantially met by granting them the maximum without separation. Because separation anywhere in the world is not a permanent solution to a problem; rather, it creates new problems.

It is a fact that non-violent ***Satyagraha*** sometimes takes a long time. However, it definitely causes less damage or no damage to persons and property; nor does it leave the trace of hatred and ill-will. Ultimately imbibed with ***Ahimsa***, it is the pursuit of truth and we all know that truth always wins.

References:

1. Mahatma, Volume-8, page 170 [Mahatma Gandhi believes, ***"Non-violence is a plant of slow growth. It grows imperceptibly, but surely. And even at the risk of being misunderstood, I must act in obedience to 'the still small voice'."***]

2. An Autobiography or The Story of My Experiments With Truth, page 383 [In this regard, he went to the extent of saying, ***"and a man who aspires after that cannot afford to keep out of any field of life. That is way; my devotion to Truth has drawn me into the field of politics; and I can say without slightest hesitation, and yet in all humility, that those who say that religion has nothing to do with my politics, do not know what religion means."***]

3. India of My Dreams, pp 63-4

4. Of Ahmedabad

5. Towards Peace, page 138

6. Of the Twentieth Century when there arose a dispute between mill-owners and labourers of Ahmedabad and Mahatma Gandhi was requested to intervene and later for arbitration; he accepted the request and made both the sides agreed upon a compromise, which later paved way to maintain relations between the two if such situation emerged again.

Bibliography:

- Gandhi, MK, An Autobiography or The Story of My Experiments With Truth, Navajivan Publishing House, Ahmedabad [India], 1927
- Kumar, Ravindra, Non-Violence And Its Philosophy, Dynamic Publications Ltd., Meerut, Uttar Pradesh [India], 2003
- Kumar, Ravindra, Towards Peace, Gyan Publishing House, New Delhi [India], 2007
- Tendulkar, DG, Mahatma: Life of Mohandas Karamchand Gandhi, Volume-5, VK Jhaveri & DG Tendulkar, Bombay, [India], 1952
- Tolstoy, Leo, The Law of Violence and The Law of Love, The Unicorn Press, London [UK], 1959

*****

7

Gandhism in Responding to Conflicts

"Sarva Dharma Sambhaava is necessary for harmony among the people belonging to different faiths or communities."

-MK Gandhi

Transformation of Conflict Without the Use of Violence; Examples of the Past; People's Approach to Gandhism in Current Perspectives; Application of Gandhism in a New Place, Especially in Local Context-in Jacksonville and at the National Level.

Gandhism and Non-Violence

Before initiating discussion pertaining to conflict resolution and Gandhism, we must first firmly keep in mind that Gandhism revolves around non-violence; Gandhism maintains its existence through non-violence and cannot stray from its domain.

Non-Violence: A Natural and Active Value

Non-violence is a natural and living value; it is the law of life. Although non-violence has been present within man from the moment of his emergence on earth, its manifestation started from the moment human beings became absorbed with thoughts of their safety. Those human beings, according to Mahatma Gandhi, were ***Rishis***[1], they were great scientists, because they ***"discovered the law of non-violence in the midst of violence"***[2] and due to this very invention, ***"...they were greater geniuses than Newton. They were themselves greater warriors than Wellington. Having themselves known the use of arms they realized their uselessness, and [after this realization they] taught the weary world that its salvation lay not through violence but through non-violence."***[3]

Non-violence is an active force and a weapon of the brave; it has nothing to do with cowardice. It does not mean meek submission to the will of the evil-doer; in Mahatma Gandhi's eyes, ***"it means pitting of one's whole soul against the will of the tyrant."***[4]

Being the law of life, an active force and a weapon of the brave, non-violence accords solutions to every problem, big or small, at all levels, in all places at all times, present or future. It transforms conflicts [having originated in violence] into cooperation [a chief feature of non-violence] and brings all parties in dispute to a win-win situation. Within this benevolent and welfaristic solution, one can neither claim to be victorious nor can the other feel defeated.

Inevitability of Disputes and Conflicts

Having acknowledged Gandhism and its affiliation with non-violence, we should also note that disputes are inevitable in human society. Conflicts, however, temporary in nature, have occurred amongst people through all ages.

My native village [Kakrauli in Muzaffar Nagar district in Northern India] has inhabitants belonging to different Castes, Sub-castes, religious-communities, races and sects. Kakrauli is an old and historical village, which is to some extent comparable to Jacksonville, a southern city in the United States, whose history is typical of race relations for the region and time, along with its neighbour St. Augustine, the oldest city in America. As I understand it, Jacksonville's approximately one million inhabitants represent Christianity, Judaism, Islam, Hinduism and Buddhism. Whites and blacks both reside here, as well as Hispanics and Asians. Hence Jacksonville is a microcosm of the world.

As a child, I witnessed many disputes with their resultant clashes occurring time and again between two persons or groups in my village. Though it happened rarely, sometimes the disputes between these groups escalated into a serious threat to the peace of the entire village by taking a communal colour, in which so many villagers would get injured and the matter would be brought to the local police. In most of these cases, the warring groups would lose their belligerence overnight. The parties involved would allow their tempers to cool, whereupon they would reach a mutually agreed-upon compromise. The compromise was either brought about by the involved parties themselves or through the efforts of respected fellow inhabitants of the village.

With the passing of time I heard about brawls and quarrels of a serious nature amongst groups within neighbouring villages, as well as between the villages themselves. I witnessed the amicable settlement of disputes between the two individuals or groups by the same method mentioned previously. In most of the cases where the disputes involved two villages, five chosen members from each village would sit and go over the entire problem and in due course strike a mutually agreed upon resolution. In some instances villages would take their disputes to the court in hopes of a victory in their favour. But in a country like India the court cases would carry on for days, months and even years. Parties involved in these disputes would tire of the legal process, which would naturally lead them into a process of dialogue. During the course of dialogue, they would reach the conclusion that a court would not be helpful at all, as the court's decision would not be in line with their wishes.

I grew up. From radio, magazines, and newspapers I grew to learn of disputes over boundaries and the sharing of river water amongst the provinces of my own country. Although these disputes were quite different in nature from the ones that arose between individuals, groups or villages, the solution to all these conflicts would be reached through the process of dialogue or negotiation. Furthermore, I found that nations involved in disputes and wars would ultimately arrive at compromise and treaties after passing through the process of dialogue and negotiation.

I have gone through the pages of world history where I can clearly observe that this process of dialogue and negotiation is an old method to resolve problems, settle disputes, transform conflicts and end wars. Gandhism is in complete agreement with this method; furthermore it adds a new dimension according to the demands of time and space by making it more comprehensive and adaptable. Gandhism is also particularly significant to Jacksonville, the largest city in the continental United States, where people of different faiths and customs reside; where a new leadership has emerged, but where old black-white relations have remained tense with the added difficulty of newly arrivals, Asians, Hispanics, etc.

Gandhism and Conflict Resolution

Gandhism generally accepts the inevitability of disputes and conflicts at different levels and in various walks of life; it calls upon people to resolve or transform these conflicts amicably through a non-violent method. Non-violence is a value permanently present in human nature as well as the basis of the conduction of society's activities. Individual and collective introspection are indispensable in understanding disputes. To go to the root of the problem it is the first step of the process that leads to the resolution and transformation of conflict, and ultimately it leads to the establishment of a fearless and peaceful order.

After introspection and going to the root cause of the dispute, the dialogue and negotiation process begins, during which the involved parties are accorded full opportunities to present their viewpoint. Many a time this proves to be the final step, the resolution of which might be:

- An individual, group, or party found guilty is asked to express regret, which, if accepted willingly, the problem or dispute is resolved; conflict is transformed; and
- The guilty, besides expressing regret is asked to compensate the aggrieved, and if it is accepted, dispute is resolved permanently.

Now, if the clash is of a fierce nature involving grievous injuries or the killing of persons, and the matter reaches police, it too can be resolved through the same process, irregardless of the time it takes for introspection [to reach the root cause of the dispute], dialogue, negotiations, or arbitration.

This is the simplest non-violent Gandhian way of resolving disputes or transforming conflicts at the individual or community level. It can also be applied to the solution of problems at the national and international level, as I have urged in my various lectures on this subject, especially during my time in Florida.

The Gandhian way, being the simplest way, may be deemed to be rough or inferior. However, it is in fact more significant today because of its belief in human unity, which when realized and accepted, brings the state of confrontation down to the lowest level.

Today, in spite of competition in every walk of life and at every level, people with their different customs, faiths and traditions are living with a continuously increasing spirit of cooperation. Due to development, literacy and an awakening consciousness, people around the world are growing closer day-by-day. So many among them have realized that the state of isolation cannot be helpful at all as we proceed on the path of progress, and that cooperation in all walks of life has become a necessity. This is why; people in large numbers are now fully capable of understanding and accepting the reality of human unity.

Role of NGO'S and Educational Institutions

Also, when people in larger numbers have known the reality of human unity, it is easier for men to resolve disputes and transform conflict through non-violent means even within the domain of established law and order. Moreover, educational institutions, non-government organizations and those concerned with human welfare can play vital roles in increasing the spirit of cooperation amongst the masses. They can impart the message of ***Sarva Dharma Sambhaava***, which according to Mahatma Gandhi, ***"is necessary for harmony among the people belonging to different faiths or communities."***[5]

This is especially true for a city like Jacksonville, where the literacy rates are satisfactory, making it possible for institutions to achieve their goal for the common cause.

Educational institutions in particular can motivate people to realize that through conflicts nothing can be achieved permanently. For, it is only within the state of cooperation that development is feasible, and if a hurdle occurs on the way to progress, it can be removed through non-violent means. Furthermore, if there is loss of wealth, property or people during the course of conflict, it is a loss to humanity as a whole.

These are the days of globalization. Everything seems to be connected now in one way or the other. At all levels and in all spheres, dependency on each other has increased so much that no one can think of living in a state of isolation. Therefore, many youth of the day acknowledge this reality. To quote one such youth who also happened to be a student of mine in Spain in 2001:

"We can see that we live in a globalize world, no one can remain isolated from each other or unaffected by changes, so it is important to develop a sprit of mutual cooperation as well as of tolerance together with the spirit of nationality and understanding."[6]

In such a situation, it is easier to make the people realize the importance and significance of non-violence and activities related to it. I am confident that educational institutions will come forward to accomplish this task of utmost importance.

The Gandhian approach in theory and in practice is before us as a guideline. Apart from adopting it in syllabi in our schools, colleges and universities, as well as to every extent possible in our regional and national circumstances, we can apply it in our daily routines individually as well as collectively. Gandhism is based upon the old rule of non-violence. In it is the call for highest morality in the form of ***"returning well for evil."***[7]

It stimulates the acceptance of reality of the oneness of all and rejects the very idea of the so-called clash of civilizations. Furthermore, it inspires self-sacrifice as the Mahatma himself said:

"There are so many causes that I am prepared to die for, but no cause that I am prepared to kill for."

The Gandhian way is welfaristic, all-timely, and as mentioned already, brings all parties in dispute to a win-win situation. It does not create a permanent solution to a dispute, in which one can claim to be victorious and the other feel defeated; rather within Gandhism both parties feel satisfied.

References:

1. Young India, 8 August 1920
2. Ibid
3. Ibid
4. Ibid [For, he further says, ***"Working under this law of our being, it is possible for a single individual to defy the whole might of an unjust empire to save his honour, his religion, his soul, and lay the foundation for that empire's fall or its regeneration."***
5. Mahatma Gandhi at the Close of...., page 2
6. Quoted from Gandhian Non-violence as an Instrument for Solving Global Conflicts [in MGACOTC, page 35]

7. Ibid, page 13

Bibliography:

- Fischer, Louis, The Life of Mahatma Gandhi, Collier Books, Toronto, [Canada], 1969
- Gandhi, MK, Young India Weekly, Volume-Two, [1920], Reprinted by Navajivan Publishing House, Ahmedabad [India], 1984
- Greg, Richard, The Power of Non-Violence, Schocken Books, New York [USA], 1959
- Kumar, Ravindra, Essays on Gandhism and Peace, Krishna Publications, Meerut, Uttar Pradesh [India], 1999
- Kumar, Ravindra, Mahatma Gandhi at the Close of Twentieth Century, Anmol Publications Pvt. Ltd. , New Delhi [India], 2004
- Kumar, Ravindra, Non-Violence And Its Philosophy, Dynamic Publications Ltd., Meerut, Uttar Pradesh [India], 2003
- Kumar, Ravindra, Towards Peace and Prosperity, World Peace Movement Trust, Meerut, Uttar Pradesh [India], 2003

****

Appendices

"To me religion means truth and Ahimsa or rather truth alone, because truth includes Ahimsa, Ahimsa being the necessary and indispensable means for its discovery."

-MK Gandhi

1

[Dangers of Democracy]

"There is no human institution but has its dangers. The greater the institution the greater the chances of abuse; democracy is a great institution and therefore it is liable to be greatly abused. The remedy, therefore, is not avoidance of democracy but reduction of possibility of abuse to a minimum.

"The Congress has become a vast democratic body. It reached a high water-mark during the past twelve months. Without being technically on the register millions took possession of it and added luster to it. But ***goondaism*** also entered the Congress to a much larger extent than hitherto. It was inevitable. The ordinary rules prescribed for the selection of volunteers were practically set aside during the last stages of the struggle. The result has been that in some places ***goondaism*** has made itself felt. Some Congressmen have even been threatened with disaster if they will not give the money demanded of them. Of course, professional ***goondas*** may also take advantage of the atmosphere and play their trade.

"The wonder is that the cases I have in mind are to very few compared to what they might have been, regarding to the great mass awakening. My conviction is that this happy state is due to the Congress creed of non-violence, even though we have but crudely followed it. But there has been sufficient expression of goondaism to warn us to take time by the forelock and adopt preventive and precautionary measures.

"The measures that suggest themselves to me are naturally and certainly a scientific and more intelligent and disciplined application of non-violence. In the first place if we had a firmer faith in non-violence than we have shown, not one man or woman who did not strictly confirm to the rules regarding the admission of volunteers would have been taken. It would be no answer to say that in that case there would have been no volunteer during the final stage and therefore there would have been a perfect failure. My experience teaches me to the contrary. It is possible to fight a non-violent battle even with one ***Satyagrahi***. But it, i.e., a non-violent battle, cannot be fought with a million non-***Satyagrahis***. And I would welcome even an utter failure with non-violence unimpaired rather than depart from it by a hair's breadth to achieve a doubtful success. Without adopting a non-compromising attitude so far as non-violence is concerned, I can see nothing but disaster in the end. For, at the critical moment we may be found wanting, weighed in the scales of non-violence, and may be found hopelessly unprepared to meet the forces of disorder that might suddenly be arrayed against us.

"But having made the mistake of indiscriminate recruiting how we are to repair the mischief in a non-violent way? Non-violence means courage of the highest order and therefore readiness to suffer. There should therefore be no yielding to bullying, bluff or worse, even though it may mean the loss of a few precious lives. Writers of threatening letters should be made to realize that their threats will not be listened to. But at the same time their disease must be diagnosed and properly treated. Even the goondas are part of us and therefore they must be handled gently and sympathetically. People generally do not take the *goondaism* for the love of it. It is a symptom of a deeper-seated disease in the body politic. The same law should govern our relations with internal *goondaism* that we apply in our relations with the ***goondaism*** in the system of Government. And if we have felt that we have the ability to deal with that highly organized *goondaism* in a non-violent manner how much more should we feel the ability to deal with the internal *goondaism* by the same method?

"It follows that we may not seek police assistance to deal with the disease although it is open during the truce, to say Congressman to seek it precisely in the same manner as any other citizen. The way I have suggested is the way of reform, conversion, love. Seeking police assistance is the way of punishment, fear, want of affection if not actual disaffection. The two methods therefore cannot run together. The way of reform appears at some stage or other to be difficult but it is in reality the easiest."

2

[Religious Education]

"To me religion means truth and ***Ahimsa*** or rather truth alone, because truth includes ***Ahimsa***, ***Ahimsa*** being the necessary and indispensable means for its discovery. Therefore anything that promotes the practice of these virtues is a means for imparting religious education and the best way to do this, in my opinion, is for the teachers rigorously to practice these virtues in their own person. Their very association with the boys, whether on the playground or in the classroom, will then give the pupils a fine training in these fundamental virtues.

"So much for instruction in the universal essentials of religion; a curriculum of religious instruction should include a study of the tenets of faiths other than one's own. For this purpose the students should be trained to cultivate the habit of understanding and appreciating the doctrines of various great religions of the world in a spirit of reverence and broad-minded tolerance. This if properly done would help to give them a spiritual assurance and a better appreciation of their own religion. There is one rule, however, which should always be kept in mind while studying all great religions and that is, that one should study them only through the writings of known votaries of their respective religions. For instance, if one wants to study the ***Bhagavata*** one should do so not through a translation of it made by a hostile critic but one prepared by a lover of the ***Bhagavata***. Similarly to study the Bible one should study it through the commentaries of devoted Christians. This study of other religions besides one's own will gives one a grasp of the rock-bottom unity of all religions and afford a glimpse also of that universal and absolute truth which lies beyond the 'dust of creeds and faiths.'

"Let no one even for a moment entertain the fear that a reverent study of other religions is likely to weaken or shake one's faith in one's own. The Hindu system of philosophy regards all religions as containing the elements of truth in them and enjoins an attitude of respect and reverence towards them all. This of course presupposes regard for one's own religion.

Study and appreciation of other religions need not cause a weakening of that regard; it should mean extension of that regard to other religions.

"In this respect religion stands on the same footing as culture. Just as preservation of one's own culture does not mean contempt for that of others, but requires assimilation of the best that there may be in all the other cultures, even so should be the case with religion. Our present fears and apprehensions are a result of the poisonous atmosphere that has been generated in the country, the atmosphere of mutual hatred, ill-will and distrust. We are constantly labouring under a nightmare of fear lest some one should stealthily undermine our faith or the faith of those who are dear and near to us. But this unnatural state will cease when we have learnt to cultivate respect and tolerance towards other religions and their votaries."

****

Who's Who

Aquino, [Ninoy] Benigno : The popular opposition senator and a leader; was husband of María Corazón Sumulong Cojuangco, popularly known as Cory Aquino, the first female President of The Philippines [1986 to 1992], was assassinated on August 21, 1983

Einstein, Albert : [March 14, 1879- April 18, 1955] was an Extraordinary Professor at Zurich in 1909; became Director of the Kaiser Wilhelm Physical Institute and Professor in the University of Berlin in 1914; was appointed Professor of Theoretical Physics at Princeton; emerged as a leading figure of the World Government Movement after the Second World War in 1945

King, Martin Luther Jr. : [January 15, 1929 – April 4, 1968] was one of the main leaders of the American Civil Rights Movement, a political activist, was awarded the Nobel Peace Prize as the youngest laureate in 1964; was assassinated in Memphis, Tennessee on April 4, 1968

Kripalani, Jivatram Bhagwandas : [188-1982] was a leading intellectual and Gandhian Socialist, environmentalist and freedom fighter; became President of the Indian National Congress at its Meerut Session in 1946

Mandela, Nelson Rolihlahla : [July 18, 918] has been a leader of Anti-Apartheid movement, remained the first democratically elected State President of South Africa between 10 May 1994 and June 1999; was conferred the Nobel Peace Prize in 1993, and the ***Bharat Ratna*** [highest Civil Award of India] in 1990

Newton, Isaac : [1642-1727], was a great mathematician, physicist and one of the foremost scientists; earned reputation as a most highly esteemed natural philosopher of Europe for his theory of gravitation; joined the University of Cambridge in 1661; was elected a fellow of Trinity College in 1667; became Lucasian Professor of Mathematics in 1669

O'Dwyer, Michael : Lt. Governor of Punjab was responsible for the Jallianwala Bagh [Amritsar] massacre of 13 April 1919, which claimed the lives of several hundred innocent Indian men, women and children; was assassinated in London on March 13, 1940

Rolland, Romain : [January 29, 1866 – December 30, 1944] was a renowned French writer, who won the Nobel Prize for Literature in 1915; his work

		Conversations with Rabindranath Tagore and Mohandas Karamchand Gandhi became famous after the Second World War as it revealed his concern for peace.
Wellington, Duke of, or Wellesley, Arthur	:	[1769-1852] was an Anglo-Irish general, statesman and the victor of the Battle of Waterloo; was appointed Chief Secretary for Ireland in 1801; became the Prime Minister of Britain twice.

****

Glossary of Indian Terms

Dharma	:	Behaviour; deeds, duty; feeling; religious injunction
Rishi	:	A sage; most learned; great scholar
Sarvodaya	:	Generally rise or development of all; one of the most important aspects of Gandhian philosophy
Tirthankara	:	Title of venerated deities in Jainism-twenty-four in number
Vedantic	:	Of the end of the *Veda*; *Upanishadic* [of *Upanishads*, which are regarded as teaching an essentially monistic doctrine]; philosophy and theology based on *Upanishads*
Vedic	:	Pertaining to Vedas-the most sacred and ancient scripture of the *Vedic-Hindus*, four in number
Vidya	:	Knowledge; learning; study; field of knowledge, science; skill or art

****

Glossary of Other Terms

Black Act	:	Proposed by the Transvaal [South Africa] Government in 1906, in which there was a provision for registration of every Indian man, woman or a child above eight years of age, and this was called a '***Black Act***' by MK Gandhi
Civil Disobedience Movement	:	The second mass ***Satyagraha*** launched by Mahatma Gandhi in 1930 by breaking the *Salt Law*
Immigration Act	:	Similar to the '***Black Act***' and proposed by the Transvaal Government in 1907
Pound-3 Tax	:	Imposed by the Natal Government [South Africa] in 1894 on every indentured Indian
Salt Law	:	The production of salt in India in those days or its procurement was not possible without paying tax to the Government; without paying tax, its production or procurement tantamounted to breaking the law, which Gandhi did in 1930 and through it started the ***Civil Disobedience Movement*** on mass scale

****

"Mahatma Gandhi's endeavours for self-realization were through strict observance of Satya [truth]. He moulded his actions on the basis of truth, only the truth that he perceived within. The word truth ordinarily connotes not to tell lies. But for Mahatma Gandhi it implied much more. Even hiding the truth from someone was deemed as untruth by him. He considered that the narrow implication of the term had belied its magnitude."

-The Author

****

Index

****